TOR and The Dark Net

Remain Anonymous and Evade NSA Spying

James Smith

CONTENTS

PART ONE: THE SECURITY MINDSET

Introduction

You are being watched.

Right now, at this moment, people you will never meet are compiling information on you, your family, your beliefs, your shopping habits, and what you might be doing a year from now.

Think carefully about everything that implies. Because the scenario described above is not a paranoid fantasy. This is the world we live in.

I want to thank you and congratulate you for downloading the book, "Tor and The Dark Net – Remain Anonymous and Evade NSA Spying." Hopefully, this will be your first step to protecting your privacy, your civil rights, and even your finances against the many digital threats we all face – and so few people are truly aware of.

Online privacy exists only in as much as you claim it by your own actions. In this day and age, if you are using a computer or device that is connected to the internet, you do not have automatic privacy. That is the simple truth; you need only to look at the user agreements for popular online services, such as Facebook or Dropbox, to realize this. The US Supreme Court has even formally ruled that no confidentiality applies to webmail because it is transmitted and stored outside of the physical control of a sender and a recipient (much like paper mail is?!). Furthermore, unscrupulous individuals, criminal gangs, and – not least – governments are all interested in what you are doing and what you have to lose. The NSA, the FBI, and sophisticated hacker groups – often allied with the traditional organized crime – have the ability to track anything and everything you are doing.

For some, this may not matter at all, as they don't care who has access to their files, data, browsing habits, or whereabouts. This only proves that many people fall into the "ostrich trap," assuming that, because a threat is mildly complicated, it can't possibly hurt them. They find the nearest convenient hole in the ground, stick their head in it, and hope for the best, right up to the moment when what they never saw coming hits them.

So, what if an identity thief obtains a loan in your name? It's the bank's problem, right? Well…no. Typically, the fraudster will get away clean, the bank's lawyers will wash their hands, and the victim will be responsible for clearing up the mess – if he doesn't have to pay back the loan he knew nothing about, too.

So, what if people know where you live? Your house isn't a secret bunker, after all. But consider a recent case of a medical doctor associated with a research institute that performs vivisection (experiments on animals, often cruel). An activist group took offense and publicized his home address, his and his wife's workplaces with telephone numbers, where their children went to school…all information voluntarily posted to social media, giftwrapped and ready for an instant harassment campaign.

So, what if the government knows all about you? They already do, anyway, from your tax returns alone. Yet, they spend more than $ 50 billion annually collecting a record of every phone call and every web interaction you make. The avowed purpose of this massive surveillance program is to keep us safe – do you feel safer now?

The good news is there are tricks and tactics you can use to insulate yourself from this. Inside this book, you will find step by step instructions and techniques that will make you completely anonymous on the internet. If used correctly, not even the NSA will be able to sniff you out. Everyone's situation and the appropriate level of security is different, so this book breaks down the available options. Based on this information, and the step-by-step guides in using them, and precise definitions of what secure features each guide offers, you will be able to choose what will work for you.

It is my hope that this book is able to inform you of all your options to remain anonymous. Thanks again for downloading your copy!

THANK YOU FOR BUYING THIS PINNACLE PUBLISHERS BOOK!

Join our mailing list and get updates on new releases, deals, bonus content and other great books from Pinnacle Publishers. We also give away a new eBook every week completely free!

Scan the Above QR Code to Sign Up

Or visit us online to sign up at
www.pinnaclepublish.com/newsletter

The Nature of the Problem

The world, as always, remains a dangerous place. Today, we need not worry about saber-tooth tigers devouring our children or the imminent threat of a nuclear holocaust, but it would be a mistake to think that our property and liberty are not exposed to new, different kinds of threats.

Drones armed with anti-tank missiles patrol the sky – perhaps not over your house, at the moment, but this little fact offers little comfort to a Pakistani widow. Infants with names similar to those of terrorists are subjected to strip-search at airports. Law enforcement donates 1,400 firearms to drug smugglers in the interest of fighting crime. The Secretary of State stores secret information on an unapproved server without getting so much as a slap on the wrist, even when this information is leaked. The government spies on newspapers, while newspapers challenge the government less and less. Spies have their secret identities revealed by their own bosses for doing their jobs; the bosses' boss reduces the sentence for a friend. At the same time, patriots who dare to embarrass the government by releasing its own information on war crimes and constitutional breaches are called traitors and persecuted so as to serve as an example to others.

> https://en.wikipedia.org/wiki/ATF_gunwalking_scandal
> https://en.wikipedia.org/wiki/Valerie_Plame#Libby_trial

In short: we are living in the information age, and the world has gone completely nuts.

If we are to face reality head-on, we have to start by acknowledging the fact that we have to protect our own right to privacy and digital security. The police will not do it for us; they can't even deal with the existing crime problem. The government is not interested in your privacy; they have different priorities, and your civil rights are just likely to get in their way. Your internet service provider will not do it for you either. We are each on our own. Aren't you glad now you picked up this book?

There are still people who spout the line "if you have nothing to hide, you have nothing to fear." It is amazing, but some people will actually fall into the "ostrich trap" with such enthusiasm that they insist everybody else join them in the sand! First of all, we all have plenty to hide. You should, under no circumstances, share your bank account, social security number or several other pieces of information with the world. What you and your significant other do behind closed doors is no business of anyone else. If you privately express an opinion about some government policy or politician, those words should go no further than the people you're talking to.

The above applies even to the averagely wholesome taxpayer who goes to church five times a month and never gets a parking ticket. However, anyone who's scanned history even a little knows that, in different times and different places, it was a very good idea to lay low if you were a Communist, a Democrat, Catholic, Protestant, Jewish, Muslim, gay, pacifist, militant, anti-slavery... completing the list would just waste ink, but the principle is clear: *matters of conscience are not always for public consumption.*

You may have any of several reasons to value your privacy. If you are a corporate officer, accountant, etc., you have a legal and ethical obligation to safeguard confidential information in your care. You may have controversial political opinions, such as about legalizing drugs – a debate that is currently roughly where the Suffragette Movement was a hundred years ago. You may be a journalist covering corruption and abuses of power, with a duty to protect your sources' privacy. You might be living in a country like Iran or China, where everything which is not permitted is forbidden.

Finally, you might just be a bad person who gets his kicks from selling cocaine and building bombs. If so, this book is not meant for you. There are probably numerous books on drugs and terrorism that you could read instead. But, at the end of the day, I cannot stop you from using technology for your twisted business, and I'm sure that you would still be doing the exact same things if you didn't have the internet.

This book is meant to inform ordinary people about the ways in which they can protect themselves from genuine threats. It will not encourage illegal or immoral behavior, and neither will it pretend that the actions of the government and its employees are always legal and moral. A government that spies on every one of its citizens, while actively concealing its own scandals, does not inspire my absolute trust.

It's the Little Things: What Everybody Should Know About Information Hygiene

Let's say you want to email your cousin in the Middle East. He might have been born there, he might have gone there to study the Koran, or he might be working for the Red Cross. The surveillance system doesn't care whether you've actually done something that warrants suspicion or not. If you tick the wrong boxes, you will be flagged for further attention. Should this escalate to the point where your entire life has been turned upside down before you are proven to be no more than a normal human being, don't expect to be told "sorry."

So, without even mentioning protection against outright theft and fraud by career criminals, you should seriously consider the necessity of protecting yourself against law enforcement (abbreviated LE in this book). The function of the police, the courts, customs and immigration control, and a double handful of inscrutable agencies with three-letter acronyms, are *not* to make the streets safe for ordinary citizens. If that were their overriding goal, the streets *would* be safe for ordinary citizens, *quod eratdemonstrandum*. What their actual individual motivations, political imperatives, and institutional goals are, is beyond the scope of this book, but try to forget your preconceptions for a moment.

Forget what you've seen on TV; that is entertainment, not information. Just because your local patrol cop is a nice guy you say hi to now and again, does not mean he won't do whatever his boss tells him to. And his boss has a boss, who has a boss, and all of them have their own interests to take care of, and none of them will lose a minute of sleep if you and yours should be robbed or murdered. On the other hand, there are plenty of stories of miscarriage of justice out there – I don't mean somewhere in the Philippine jungle, I mean close to where you live. Worse, it can only be called a "miscarriage of justice" if the wrongfully accused party can absolutely, unequivocally prove his innocence; otherwise, it's "justice" by definition. There may be many, many innocent people in jail we don't know about.

So, rather than relying on LE to protect you, you might need to protect yourself from LE. With all your internet and telephonic connections monitored and recorded, this amounts to (a) not arousing suspicion, and (b) if suspicion is somehow aroused, not allowing it to be connected to your real identity. As shown in the example that opened this chapter, judicial suspicion has nothing to do with moral guilt. Your job (journalist, investigator, lawyer, academic) may require you to access information a "plain vanilla" citizen might not need to. Unlike the "plain vanilla" stereotype, who worries mostly about his next car payment, you might feel passionate about financial regulatory reform, ecological issues, or not supporting a war on foreign soil. These are your rights and, as many would argue, your duty. People have also been placed under surveillance for doing exactly that.

https://www.aclu.org/other/top-ten-abuses-power-911

So, before we jump right in and start learning to use the TOR anonymous network, let's review a few best basic practices for securing your information and privacy online. This helps us make a start at developing what I will call a security mindset, which is simply the realization that information can hurt you, and that it is your own responsibility to guard against that risk.

- FORGET about your online privacy being automatic. It just isn't, unless you take the steps we will describe in the following chapters. Your email, search engine requests, instant messages: they are ALL in a format that can be easily intercepted by an interested party.

- It is highly recommended that you use multiple identities online for different things. In the jargon of security engineering, a shared credential is only as strong as its weakest link. If your bank allocated your account number and PIN by your phone number...well, you get the idea. Perhaps, if you are a buyer and a seller on an infamous bazaar, you will want to have separate credentials for these separate roles. And then possibly a third login for your favorite forum. Equally, you should still use a different username and password for your corporate login, another for your webmail, and so on. In the first place, if an attacker manages to hack one identity, the others remain intact. In the second place, see the previous paragraph. People with bad intentions towards you can analyze your network traffic. If they see a js833 logging on to rainforestIntervention.com, a jim_s posting on frackingDestroysNature.org, a jsmith.hr@company.com sending an email to a client, and a Jimmy S. replying to a memo to his yoga class…you get the picture. James Smith is already a known quantity, an open book. At the very least, clearly separate your social, activist, and professional personas.

- Know the absolute basics about internet security. This is no more than basic computer literacy. Delete spam without opening, even if it does promise you more money, sex, and happiness than you could possibly want. Update your security software regularly. Don't download email attachments you aren't expecting. Know that your wife's birthday is not a secure password; neither is any word found in the dictionary.

- Don't fall victim to "social engineering."[1] If someone you don't recognize phones you claiming to be from your bank and asks you to confirm the first and last digit of your credit card number, your bullshit detector *should be howling*. The only correct approach is to give the caller a succinct and pointed analysis of his character, and immediately get into contact with your bank. Otherwise, any successful attack will be *your* — instead of *their* — problem.

- Just because millions of people use a given internet service does not mean *you* should trust it implicitly. Do your research about what their policies actually mean for user's rights (definitely including copyright). It's not uncommon for even major, technologically sophisticated organizations to be hacked and their customers' data released, so be careful what you share.

- A common hacker trick is to provide infrastructure, then monitor traffic passing over it for financial information

---

[1] "Social engineering" is when a hacker tricks a victim into giving up confidential information, usually by pretending to be someone else or phishing. Most hacks are accomplished in this way.

and passwords. *Never* use a free Wi-Fi network for anything more personal than a weather report.

- The intended recipients can see your messages. They don't need to know if you are currently online, what your time zone is, or anything else you don't feel like sharing. For any online service you use, check the *Account Settings* (or similar) page and see if your privacy is being protected.

- Learn to be suspicious. Your grandmother might have said "you can't go through life never trusting people," but, at least online, she would have been wrong. No matter how slick an online store looks, no matter how many corporate logos they have on their payment portal, think twice before trusting them with your credit card details. And if they only, for instance, accept payments through Western Union, *IT...IS...A...SCAM.*

- Treat any information you post online as if the whole world will see it. Do you really want everybody to know how much you earn, how drunk you got last Saturday, and what you really think of your manager? This advice goes double for social media. If your actions or beliefs are in any way controversial, expect LE to read every word you type (and remember, in the past, "controversial" could have meant being a Mormon, supporting equal rights for people regardless of skin color, or opposing an undeclared war on the other side of the world).

- Get informed about your browser's security settings. For starters, disable cookies and JavaScript unless you actually need that functionality (we will be speaking about this in more detail later).

Bonus Tails Installation Guide

Installing tails can be a challenging and confusing task. There are a few caveats to doing it correctly and safely. I have taken the time to compile a tutorial with step-by-step instructions on how to install tails on a USB drive with persistence. Installing it with persistence is important because it allows you to store important information on an encrypted part of the drive that will remain there even when tails wipes itself clean. The fact that it is encrypted is good as well because no one can see the stored information.

Sign up below to my email list, and I will immediately send you the FREE setup guide. You will also gain access to my email list, and I will send you information on the latest safety and anonymity practices!

Direct Link - http://www.pinnaclepublish.com/a/link/tails-setup/

TOR AND THE DARK NET

PART TWO: GET THE TOOLS TO DO THE JOB

Encryption: What You Need to Know

This book is not intended for computer wizards; they already know what they need to. My intention is to show ordinary people the tools they need to secure their own privacy, not leave them bored and confused. However, for *security mindset* to be effective, you will need some basic information to help you think. I promise I won't burden you with more than you really need to know.

IP Addresses

IP stands for Internet Protocol, so an IP address is exactly that: a computer's address on the internet. It is expressed as a number, such as 192.168.0.1. Some IP addresses are permanently leased and assigned, such as 74.125.224.72 for Google. Try entering that number preceded by "http://" and followed by "/"; you should reach Google's homepage. If you type "www.google.com" instead, your computer first contacts a different server to ask what number goes with that name, which is used only because it's easier to remember.

Your IP address is most likely assigned to you by your internet service provider (ISP) every time you log on. Since all the internet communication goes from one IP address to another IP address, whoever you are communicating with (and whoever helps in transmitting your traffic along the way) can see your IP address. This enables them to see, amongst other things, your general geographical location.

Encryption

A lot of people smarter than me have written huge books on this subject, so let's just focus on what is essential to the user.

An encrypted message (which can be an email, or part of an internet communication, or a file on your hard drive) is one other people cannot read without the password or key. It *is* possible to break encryption to read the message anyway. It is also possible to fly to the moon by flapping your arms really hard; it's a matter of relative difficulty. Generally, if you take reasonable care, you can trust encryption.

Encryption comes in two flavors: symmetric and public-private key. Symmetric encryption uses the same key for locking and unlocking messages:

Just like the lock on your front door. Public-private key encryption is a little more complex: it uses a lock with *two* keys. If the lock is locked with the public key, only the private key can unlock it. Vice versa, if the lock has been locked with the private key, you need the public key to open it:

You might be thinking: "Well, that's a stupid lock; I'll never be able to get into my house that way." Actually, for computers on a network, it is extremely useful.

Think about a public key that all your friends have copies of and can lock mailboxes that are intended for you. Anyone can lock your mailbox, but you are the only one with the key to unlocking the box. Even if the person who sent you a message locked a message into a box with your public key, they, themselves, cannot unlock it. Only the person possessing the private key can unlock it. So, when you unlock it, you can be sure that the message inside was intended for you personally, and nobody could have changed the contents since the box was locked.

If you wish to respond to this person, you must use *their* public key to encrypt the message you want to send to them. And they use their own private key to decrypt the message you sent them.

That's the first use of public-private key cryptography. There is another that's also widely used, called authentication. Let's say I have an important document, like a will, and I want no doubt as to its authenticity. So, I use my private key (instead of someone else's public key) to lock the box. Sometime later, someone finds the box labeled "Encrypted by James Smith." All my friends have a copy of my public key, so they try it in the lock, the box opens, and they can read the message inside. "Well, it opened with James's public key," they say to themselves, "so, it had to be James who locked it in the first place, and nobody could have changed the message without his private key, so the message has to be genuine."

If you are still with me, well, there you are! This is asymmetric or public-private key cryptography and was designed so that anybody intercepting your message traffic could not decrypt the message without your private key. Even if you, yourself, lose your private key, there is no method of key recovery. You can consider that message locked forever.

Now, you will never do these calculations by hand. You will ask the computer to do it for you occasionally, but actually computers communicate with each other like this all the time. They use authentication to make sure the servers they are talking to are who they say they are; they use encryption to hide sensitive information; they do this many times every day without the user even being aware of it. So, now you know.

TOR Basics

Now, we get to the practical stuff: measures you can take to protect your information and yourself from prying eyes and sticky fingers. First and foremost, to protect yourself while browsing the internet, you should be using TOR, which stands for The Onion Router. TOR will provide you with a degree of anonymity by using a 128-bit AES (Advanced Encryption Standard). There has been some debate as to whether or not the NSA can crack this code, and the answer is: probably, assuming they are willing to spend the time and resources. This is why you should never send anything over TOR that you aren't comfortable sharing with the entire world unless you are using some sort of further encryption (which we will talk about later).

How TOR works:

Ordinarily, if we're talking about transmission, "the internet" means all the interlinked computers between you and your message's recipient.

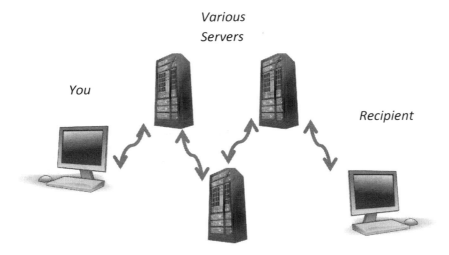

The arrows are colored green, to represent unencrypted, insecure, clear text communication links. *Every server along the path your data travels can see what you are saying, who you are saying it to, and who you are* (via your IP address).

TOR addresses this issue by the "onion" analogy. Put simply, your original message is locked in a cryptographic box, this box is locked into another box, and so on until you have layers of encryption similar to the layers of an onion. As you send the outside box to the first server in the queue (and they will all be "trustworthy" TOR servers, more on that later), it unlocks only the first box, which reveals information about where to send the box inside. The second server unlocks the second box to see where to send the third box and so on, until the final box is unlocked, revealing the IP address of the recipient.

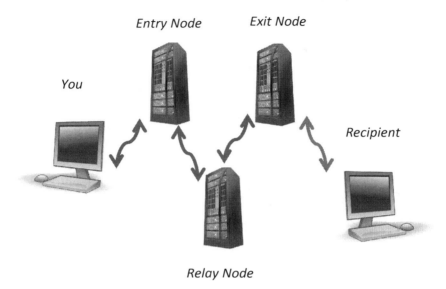

Entry Node   *Exit Node*

You

Recipient

Relay Node

Now the transmissions within the TOR network are colored red for encrypted; unreadable as far as content or addressing goes.

Communication from your computer to the internet relies on an "entry node" which is basically your computer's door into the TOR network. This entry node communicates with your computer; this entry node knows your IP address. The entry node then passes your encrypted request to the relay node(s). The relay node communicates with the entry node and the exit node but does not know your computer's IP address or the content of your messages. The exit node is where your request is decrypted and sent to the "normal" internet. The exit node does not know your computer's IP, only the IP of the relay node. Using this model of 3 nodes it makes it harder but not impossible to find a correspondence between your request and your original IP address; in any real signal path, there will usually be many more nodes involved. The actual, mathematically estimated figure is that there is a 1 in 1 to 2 million chance of your IP address being identified.

Problems arise, obviously, when you are entering plain text into TOR since anybody can set up an exit node. The FBI can set up an exit node, and so can any foreign government, the mafia, or any malicious person who may want to steal your information. You should not be entering any critically confidential data into any website, even when accessing them over TOR. If any of the nodes in the chain are compromised (and some certainly are), and the people in charge of those compromised nodes have the computing power to decrypt your request, then they *will* be able to see what you are saying.

So, what can we do to fix this? Well, luckily the TOR network contains more and more servers that are offering something called *hidden services*. You can easily recognize these services by the address **[something].onion**. These services offer what's called end-to-end encryption, from your own computer's internet connection up to whatever server you're dealing with. What this does is short-circuit the vulnerability of the possibly compromised exit node and put control back into your hands. The web server of the hidden service now becomes your exit node, which means the website you are visiting is the one decrypting your message, not some random exit node that might be under the control of an attacker. Remember, the exit node has the key to decrypt and reveal your original request. The exit node, as well as the final recipient, can see what you are sending in clear text once they decrypt it. So, if you are entering your name and address into a field, the exit node has your information. If you are supplying information such as a credit card or bank account number, your real name, or even your login information, then you are compromising your identity.

Another measure you can take is to visit only websites that use *HTTP Secure*, whether you are working through TOR or the insecure internet. You can tell if the website you are visiting is using HTTP Secure by the prefix at the beginning of the address. If you see **https://** then your website is using HTTP Secure. What this does is to encrypt your requests so that only the server can decrypt them, and not somebody eavesdropping on your communication, such as a compromised TOR exit node or your ISP. This is another form of end-to-end encryption. If somebody were to intercept your request over HTTP Secure, they would see encrypted data and would have to do a good deal of work to decrypt it.

Another reason you want to use HTTPS whenever possible is that malicious TOR entry and exit nodes can damage or change the contents of the messages passing through them and even inject malware into the connection. This is made easier when you are sending requests in plain text, but HTTPS reduces this possibility. You must still be aware, however, that HTTPS can also be currently cracked depending on the cryptographic strength of the key used to encrypt it. When you visit a website using HTTPS, you are encrypting your request using their public key, and they are decrypting it using their private key. Think of the "locked box" analogy again. A public key is automatically given to whoever wants to send an encrypted message, and the only one who can decrypt is the one with the carefully-guarded private key.

Unfortunately, many websites today are still using private keys that are only 1,024 bits long. At present, never mind next year and the one after that, this is no longer sufficient. So, you need to make sure you find out what level of encryption the website you are visiting uses, which should be a minimum of 2,048, if not 4,096 bits. Sadly, even if such protection is in place, the connection *in tor* might not be secure if have another problem. What happens if the web server itself has become compromised? Maybe your TOR nodes are all functioning perfectly, maybe you have used HTTPS for all your requests, but the actual web server hosting the website you are visiting has been compromised. Well, then all your requests are, again, as good as plain text. This kind of exploit is rare, but it is an important part of security mindset to bear in mind that it can indeed happen. So, remember that if you are a user of the Deep Web or any other form of activism, you never want to enter any identifying details about yourself online.

Make it so that even if the NSA intercepted and decrypted your internet traffic, or compromised the website you are accessing, that the only information they have about you is your username and password. How safe are that username and password? Does your username contain any personally identifiable information? Is it the same password that you use for your personal email? Does it contain a name of somebody you know personally? Always keep all of these factors in mind.

The good news is, now that you're using TOR you've already made a great leap forward regarding security. Why not try a few TOR search engines, such as Ahmia (**msydqjihosw2fsu3.onion**), Torch (**http://xmh5752oemp2sztk.onion**) or Not Evil (**http://hss3uro2hsxfogfq.onion**). Be aware, just like on the regular internet, you will be able to find content that is offensive, fraudulent or illegal. I'm going to assume that you are a responsible adult capable of using some common sense.

TORring it up Further: PGP, Tails, and Virtual Boxes

Another necessary security measure, especially when communicating over the Deep Web, is using PGP encryption. This is not always possible, such as when you are logging into a website, filling out a form, logging into an email service, and so forth (in this case https should be in place). Consider any data you enter into a website using plain text possibly compromised. Do not put anything confidential in any type of plain text online under any circumstances. PGP stands for **Pretty Good Privacy** and has been used successfully for years now. At one point, it was actually illegal to export the technology from the United States, until LE cottoned on to the idea that smuggling out mathematical formulas is not that difficult, law or no law. Perhaps, at some point, the Powers That Be will figure out that trying to implement laws that are stupid, pointless, and unenforceable only serves to detract from the authority of sensible laws that have the good of the community in mind.

In a nutshell, PGP is an easy way to turn clear text into a secure message you can share with your friends. PGP comes into play because it uses a very strong form of encryption, and is useful for encrypting, decrypting, and signing texts, e-mails, files, directories, and whole disk partitions, and increases the security of e-mail communications.

For more technical users, it uses a serial combination of hashing, data compression, symmetric-key cryptography, and finally public-key cryptography. For those more interested in how to use it than how it works, the process of encrypting messages using PGP is as follows. You create a private key and a public key. The public key is the key you give out to people you want to send you encrypted messages, or want to know if your digitally signed messages are genuine. This public key is often posted on a personal website.

Your private key is kept secret by you alone. This private key is the only key that can unlock messages that were previously locked with your public key and sent to you. If this doesn't make much sense yet, try and review the *chapter* **Encryption: What You Need to Know.**

So how do you use PGP and TOR?

Well, we're nearly there, but first, I want to introduce you to the concept of a **Live Operating System**, which adds a great deal of security while browsing the web and makes using PGP very easy. A live operating system is an operating system that you can run on top of your current operating system. If you like, it's an application that can run other applications. So, for example, there are two options if you are a Windows user. You may download the live operating system, burn it to a CD or DVD, and then boot your computer from that DVD or CD. This will make your computer run as if you have this operating system installed on your computer. However, if you remove the CD or DVD and reboot, then your computer will boot as normal. You can also use a USB drive to perform this same feature.

Secondly, you can run this live operating system in what's called a Virtual Box. Think of this as a computer that runs inside your computer and isolates it from certain online attacks. The benefits of this are that you can run Windows simultaneously as you run this other operating system, and you can easily switch back and forth between them without rebooting the computer. Both methods have their pros and cons. The most important benefit of running a live CD boot is that it reduces the risk of having your computer compromised by viruses, malware, and keyloggers that rely on Windows' vulnerabilities to run.

If you are going to run this OS from a Virtual Box, I suggest

downloading Virtual Box from Oracle. Note the **https://**

https://www.virtualbox.org/

Next, the live operating system we are going to learn to use is called **Tails**. Tails can be found at the following website.

https://tails.boum.org/

The reason I chose Tails is that it has many of the security features that you require to stay anonymous already installed. Like everything in life, Tails is not perfect, but it really is a good operating system with a strong focus on security. We will be using many of its built-in features in the following chapters, such as PGP encryption and decryption. Make sure you download the Tails ISO file from the official Tails website. Afterward, you can either load it into Virtual Box, or burn it to a DVD, or load it onto a USB, and boot your computer from that drive.

There are sufficient online tutorials on loading Tails into Virtual Box so I won't go into much detail here. I *do* have one important suggestion, though: make sure you run Virtual Box and Tails from a USB drive or SD card. I would prefer an SD card for reasons I will explain later. But, essentially, when Virtual Box runs directly on your hard drive, it creates a virtual hard drive that it uses as a temporary storage space while Tails is running. When Tails exits, this virtual drive is deleted, but that doesn't mean it is gone. As anyone who has used file recovery tools knows, deleted files are easily recoverable with the right tools. I will talk about how to protect your supposedly deleted files from data recovery tools in later chapters, but for now, just keep Virtual Box and Tails OFF of your hard drive and load it either on a USB drive or SD card. This is especially important if there is any chance of physical theft or confiscation of your computer.

The same goes when booting your computer directly into the Tails operating system from a DVD or USB stick. Your hard drive may be used to store files used by Tails, so make sure any files that Tails saves or accesses are stored on a USB stick or SD card. Otherwise, they will be recoverable. This is why I prefer using a Virtual Box and running both the Virtual Box (and Tails inside of it) off of a USB stick. Keep as much as possible off of your actual hard drive. It is possible to shred files beyond recovery, but it's much easier to do this on a 16 GB flash drive than it is a 1 TB hard drive.

Once you have Tails running on your Virtual Box, we are ready to explore using PGP. The reason we had to take a slight detour into Tails territory is that we will be using Tails for many of the features from here on out, including PGP.

The core functionality of PGP is all about keys, so let's start by creating your own! For PGP, which uses public-private key encryption, keys come in public/private pairs. Half of your personal key will consist of your public key that you can give out to people or post on your profiles online. As mentioned before, this is the key people will use to encrypt confidential messages before sending them to you. The other half of your personal key consists of your private key, which you can use to decrypt messages that are encrypted using your PGP public key.

Open the OpenPGP applet. If you look up to the top right area, you will see a list of icons, and one of them looks like a clipboard. You need to click on this icon and click **Manage Keys**

Next click **File** -> New
Select PGP Key and click Continue
Fill out your full name (I suggest you use your online name, not your real   name)
Optionally fill out an email and a comment as well.
Next, click Advanced Key Options.

Make sure Encryption Type is set to RSA and set Key Strength to 4096.
Once you have done this, click Create, and it will generate your key.

You can view your personal key by clicking the tab **My Personal Keys**. You have now created your personal key! To find your PGP public key, you right-click on your personal key and click Copy, and it will copy your PGP public key to your clipboard, in which you can paste anywhere you wish. A PGP public key will look something like this.

——BEGIN PGP PUBLIC KEY BLOCK——
mQINBFLLWDcBEADEzn3mnLsezUDDAS5Q0lm1f6JdkI534
WPuRlAN8pnuQsCSwUQUhPEAgNCUNhxN4yCJ1mDt9xpXpX8
QzsMIcofCHeE9TMLAnHzbmXLLi+D8sPZpLpDN6jEIFvmBD4
dvp5adimvRl8Ce49RpO345VUz8Ac0qLSmsv2u+kQviDQXZkrrxX
HnA
IalvgDopXTISa9Sh7J3HHYYQazOZt9mfAjjuuRdaOqmAAtEe9dl4
3nrx+nSd/fqH13XvMKhqJhIoJ02CBFfRBm86vtx5yiXqHZX438M
9kbASqU0A2jAfRd+IZG5Z9gCIW6FTror+F4i+bEdAuGTG1XFs
QSgjKTIG0vgYiTJ93C2MZxrLvNnJp0g2zD0URyk8Y2IdyCDfIL10
W9gNMqLmjD0z/f/os66wTJkflSGaU9ZsrKHUKFN5OSfOZtNqk
tWnfCpY4bigkJ8U/5C8mtr9ZE3Tv+RV4rPY0hAOtZucnhlRmYK
VFNjvbS0MjqA1188cwzBNG0XcpCNtmM5UsSvXwnDoUaEMXe
50Hikxdk3d+CJzqYnor72g/WmIDROCiXl62D9rJ2JuLpl9bQLM+
KCbXJf3kUSvzszZGXL/AwmynvqlruaXqr5975sCdfqXVexx1sxsLo
fOzE01xSDEJRWwHQPlxTKPZFnXD709Xumjdinjv1w4onLk04Z
96wARAQABtC5Kb2xseSBSb2dlciAoVGhleSB3b3VsZCBsaXZlZlIIG
FuZCBkaWUgdW5kZXIgaXQpiQI3BBMBCgAhBQJSy1g3AhsDB
QsJCAcDBRUKCQgLBRYCAwEAAh4BAheAAAoJEPuh6tSg81ny
zNsP/2ayrAz4InCK/ZnyRnnsjSHIXMv7t2uDTbYomA/0B6v/S6w
HMNZXG6+sYg41mfMuZEimgavNb0Uc2r6mI7UyWy5lp1Gd/D
+all81X7bm5EBpvl1isPgJEqjehEdh9FQjrTiRIJafM1m254hIAaZ1R
vAphI0tM2lpudk+tNKq+ivV8PpsN9TP0mg5ZAu1lIKtG9k5vS9H
AQ0grJ01TFMEjlifrf7eRyJ1+dmRJ+Xtoy2js8UwS+wMRrIi3G39P2
BfEZFQka3EmQ2JgN4pDWFoI0hODGhTba8Z0XSnVtabOTi1T
OWIFmFuyqA9bNtuOt3KhIC/O+mEATRsc/VPbTY+80kf45Lwl
DBfKO3PcOXSOG7ygibzEqXnMs/Rfe1kNEBeR9Wx2NMJSdxyp
qGij17CLJwNLC3KypTIQrhzy3YAndeDG4TadW2Pv/FJxhz+MX
+s+9VeX2fGC0Fsfp8JbeWMAznp8Rf6O/tzEYW+pbLoLRPdi/D
vFBZVyWGPspzt3Qspm+BHbeW9iFjvCyvP2/DrKmQM7ABuRh
/TMZR7uQ5na11L8rf3nzrSAl/lSul42xLzxG+h9mDixXd1Vh6rVG
MbCjL7wO25TUneFo13U5J+klo1blQWV/DLFZUwhh2utWNCM
CtcdRW0HYa14Wdyy7H68WmsJqBWUsbyD9PZ2gSawBy7uQINB
FLLWDcBEACg3IOme+sg0OZN349UYRr9/O6uW2vC5x9/azZrF

NSNYh/LFJTt3XI/FsjNgCj6NxRxbfdyLjL1gxSlJyFtclkFGS0lC0GI
z7lINvemkewjde/bHXChz2IIaIliL2A6Z6w3fP4jlQCw8NoGGJ360
WMkZVTDDakYYkb50BrZSx4TVLjrHfFuLMXTE255gQrId02jY
O6240EDIhHITuiSwUQvHtXlOrHSohN83TD1I4H7iH/FLae9gYh
4C/IxVLkzLUqvpf72Q/xogCZAJl4WEMmWD6dXufvyvhCXQnbji
LuAdQas0ef/t652LPw/vJFDSDmguw9PXWpv3vFOe13UNU//+n
w3kIGxaVWGvazXk8IFiDv9USgEGjcNn4zo8HQlQrYz9/gyI3Xoj
GV6L8iecWpHSweqR3NxKJmWKWEG1wwnWPL8M+z6OwEvR
dxVspy+eG0Zs+6igbw3tk6gJ4cq5ehdlmD6py27AhRhlj7uLlZxmK3
uFV19QjtX/Dyt73ZNX16krXqufl0HAJRd1PwhITPCtSviW3L2qK
F2Pdak3j97A656EcInCcAyOUC/mUNUDtXJik6uwFgFFn9/pnFr+
acY7ppsWPG5rr7jRj+Lgjnjkckpkjo8jN1hZE17CfJyrYrSqdglCcIgT
HteIEZdPfPUmnbbSoyeufkyEW1AoIKatQARAQABiQIfBBgBCg
AJBQJSy1g3AhsMAAoJEPuh6tSg81ny4nIP/2lVf0DTp1n5xPEBZE
UlgzcMNeh5FTIS3J44g5a+OlkRVgHFtu7K/MUsftlUzkvMMa0sXll
hKc6syxcytoD7LAt9tbQh62yEzijTliU2QFgWJSS6IfbtC2IyRouAns3
KD6XouKTFUs/i0n/QpwhnM+Ya/SAgc/oroM7SE/T4g+v6EeR
Cq7In/TMgc74j+25zUF1rVSCenbZKkYezxqZ33cXLwl7lIUBcK2u
NHDBUB5G853NR0OkBm5i+KC8vM3K1/MZ+P/lK0xOcTGX
ZH/A7GrEsI4FJnw5i6zJZb8gmDt44Tp/1Ujxnm5xhVWgnOQeSV
SyiRsHQ/gTCL1PqsZhW7yulwL05yxZgN+oYVx4pNtLJMigRjoCY
9IKEmZhY75cWXXA19j14Wnxu8IrwwSk1WyzMQcjj7onP4OEhb
PuotqWqVAc0M/+MV5oMGIG0Qepy6XpZOCCpZw/p1rDrZSY
P5eQMd/4xLB7xch6GjbWsnKhA1wGdjdclBodixorVfCRn4s5jTgX
x7wWz/opM4ix/CPAkify74Sf0BdJ5YtFILZc5StED4WC5pljJbdEW
Vsb9rn6egvFn7W/ZlDJAerS6Mt5LJGAhAude0Kz2HJwDtOBF4n
XeTzRCK5BrBnCYPHAtO2aqfowirzjMTd9A/ADoPmIbIJAm04m
A6krRiH909Bnx=Az2N
——END PGP PUBLIC KEY BLOCK——

Very importantly, you will have to save the private key on a secondary USB drive or SD card. If you are running Tails from a USB drive, then you must use a separate drive to store your key on. If you are running Virtual Box, you want to **right-click** on the icon in the bottom right corner that looks like a USB drive and select your separate drive that you will be using to store your keys on. Again, never store your private keys on your hard drive; keep them OFF your computer. The best security software in the world won't help you if you are careless with your private key.

To save your private key, you are going to right-click on your personal key and select Properties. I know you already saw the Export function, but this is not what we want. Clicking export will ONLY export your public key and will not preserve your private key. If you lose your private key, you can never recover it even if you create another personal key using the exact same password. Each private key is unique to the time it was created, and if lost, you will need NSA-style computing power to recover it. So, once you have clicked **Properties**, go over to the tab **Details** and click **Export Complete Key**.

With this done, you have saved your personal key to use again whenever you start Tails. Remember that Tails is not installed on your hard drive, so every time you restart Tails, you lose all your data, which hasn't been explicitly saved. By saving your keys onto a USB drive or SD card, you can import your keys for use whenever needed.

Next, you are going to want to learn how to encrypt and decrypt text messages and emails using your key. Tails already hasan excellent tutorial on how to do this so I will refer you to their webpage:

https://tails.boum.org/doc/encryption_and_privacy/gpgapplet/public-key_cryptography/index.en.html

But before you go look at that, I should mention that you need to find somebody else's PGP public key, or you can practice by using your own. In any case, the way you import other people's keys into what's called your **key ring** is by loading them into a text file. You do this with the Tails' program called **gedit Text Editor**.

Click Applications -> Accessories ->gedit Text Editor and enter in someone's public key (using copy and paste, not typing the whole thing a character at a time!) and hit save. Next, you can return to your key program from the clipboard icon and click File -> Import and select that file. It will import that person's public key into your keyring. To add additional public keys on your keyring, I suggest reopening the same file and just adding the next key below the previous key; each time you open that file, it will load all keys within that file. This way, you can keep all the PGP public keys you regularly use together in one file saved on your SD card or USB drive.

If you need some further information, look up

https://tails.boum.org/doc/encryption_and_privacy /gpgapplet/decrypt_verify/index.en.html

Now that you have PGP figured out (hopefully), I want to remind you that using PGP whenever possible is very important. In the online world, privacy is not a sometime thing. It is really all or nothing; it's either you care about your information becoming public, or you don't.

One of the reasons why I would suggest for you to store your PGP keys and other sensitive data on an SDcard is in case that day comes when you are compromised, and you get a knock at your door. This may never happen (and hopefully won't), but it has happened to innocent people in the past and will happen to others in future. Should you be one of the unlucky ones, you might have time to get rid of that portable storage quickly. Even better, if you have a micro SD card that plugs into an SD adapter, then you can snap it with your fingers or at the very least hide it. USBs would need to be crushed pretty thoroughly, and it might not be possible to do this in the heat of the moment, so do what seems best to you. But always keep in mind that, one day, that knock on the door might be for you.

As mentioned, PGP has been around for a while, yet a surprising number of people don't know about its existence. Talk to your friends; explain the benefits of privacy (and if you also happen to mention my book, I won't hold it against you). One may want to find out more about legal tax avoidance strategies without broadcasting the fact; another might not want uniformed strangers to read his letters to his girlfriend. Whatever the reason, privacy and data security have a place in everyone's life, and PGP is one of the best tools around.

Additional FacTORs

At this point, you understand the need to protect your privacy; you have a general idea of how TOR and PGP works, and you've set up your virtual box. This is already a decent accomplishment for one day, but it's hardly enough to ensure full protection.

Combining TOR with a VPN

A Virtual Private Network is when two networks (or at its simplest, two computers) that are physically separate, form one logical network using an encrypted connection. For example:

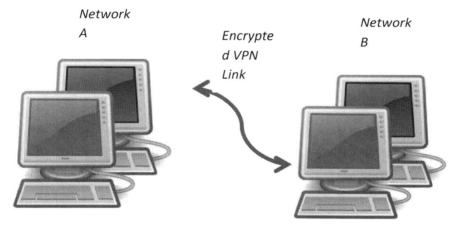

Network A   Encrypte d VPN Link   Network B

In this example, a computer physically connected to Network B can talk to a computer in Network A as if they were on the same LAN. But for privacy purposes, a VPN is often used to hide your IP address from prying eyes

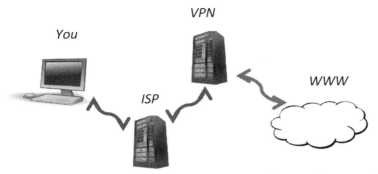

In this way, your internet service provider can't see what data you're sending or to whom, and the World Wide Web sees your traffic as coming from the VPN server's IP address. If you are surfing the internet without using TOR, you should certainly at least be using a VPN (also called a re-router). If your connection to the VPN is not encrypted (green arrows instead of red), the usefulness is much less, since some internet service providers monitor your activity to some extent. The worst example of an insecure network is public Wi-Fi, which you should not even consider using without a VPN.

There are a number of different VPNs to choose from, from "free" services that support themselves by injecting advertisements into websites (don't use any of these), to others dedicated to bypassing internet censorship laws in repressive countries, to purely commercial services. Choosing a VPN that uses at least 128-bit encryption like TOR is minimum good practice and will stop the majority of eavesdroppers. But if you can get 256-bit encryption, that is what you should go for. While doing your homework on VPN providers, you will most likely come across two protocols to choose from, PPTP and OpenVPN. Find out which one your VPN provider is using before you sign up with them. At this time, I am going to highly recommend that you avoid PPTP and stick with OpenVPN providers. Check out this site for a quick comparison.

http://www.goldenfrog.com/vyprvpn/openvpn-vs-pptp

As you can see, PPTP uses a weaker encryption, 128-bit versus 160-bit to 256-bit for OpenVPN. The older PPTP offers basic security versus a high level of security using something called digital certificates. This is basically a way to make sure the data coming in is sent from your VPN provider and not injected by some malicious third party, by having the incoming and outgoing data signed using specially obtained certificates identifying the sender.

PPTP has largely been abandoned by those who demand the highest level of securityso I would recommend avoiding it. A third option for VPN providers is L2TP/IPsec, but most experts now believe it has already been compromised by the NSA due to its weaker levels of encryption and should be avoided. **Stick with OpenVPN.**

Before we get into the subject of whether or not we should be using a VPN together with TOR, I want to give you a few warnings regarding VPN use.

If you are going to be using a VPN for any type of activism, make as sure as you can that your VPN does not keep logs. This is actually a lot harder than you might think. Many VPN providers will claim to not keep logs of your activityin order toattract your business because they have to compete with the other providers out there. Customers are going to trend towards providers who offer no identifying data retention. There is no technical or security reason for retaining *any* usage logs on a VPN server. Others claim that logs are automatically deleted after 24 hours. Unfortunately, this claim of theirs is impossible for a user to verify, and I will give you an example.

There is a well-known VPN provider named HideMyAss that previously claimed not to keep logs of its users. Unfortunately, when met with a court order from their government in Britain, they quickly provided authorities with evidence against a suspected hacker from the internet group LulzSec, which helped lead to his arrest. The story can be found below.

http://www.theregister.co.uk/2011/09/26/hidemya ss_lulzsec_controversy/

One of the take-home quotes from this article is the following.

"We are not intimidated by the US government as some are claiming, we are simply complying with our countries legal system **to avoid being potentially shut down and prosecuted**

ourselves."

You should realize that, whether in the online or offline world, nobody is going to be eager to go to jail for you. When choices like these have to be made, no VPN provider is going to risk jail to protect the identity of a $20 a month subscriber. That the VPN is not guilty of any criminal wrongdoing is beside the point. No matter how tough they sound in their marketing material, and no matter how much they claim to care about their customers, when faced with the decision to either give you up or go to jail, they will always choose their own freedom over yours.

Bearing all this in mind, the question is:

Should I use a VPN alongside TOR?

Should I use TOR to connect to a VPN, or use a VPN to connect to TOR?

Using a VPN to Connect to TOR

A VPN does hide your internet activity from your internet service provider. It can also hide the fact that you are using TOR, a practice that could raise some suspicion when the feds start asking ISPs to provide data about their users. This may or may not be relevant since many people use TOR, you can argue there are many legitimate reasons for doing so, and there is nothing inherently illegal about using the internet in this way. Still, it is just another factor that can arouse suspicion that may or may not be important to you but should be thought of, nonetheless. It is a stated NSA policy to pay more attention to spying on encrypted traffic.

So, if you connect to your VPN by first using TOR, your ISP would only be able to see that you are connecting to TOR nodes and that you are sending encrypted data. The VPN would not be able to see what data you are sending within TOR unless they decrypted it because, as you know, all information relayed over TOR is encrypted.

There are downsides, of course. Each layer of security – TOR, VPNs, end-to-end encryption – adds a little to your network *latency*, or how long it takes for a request to be processed. Also, as mentioned, VPN servers may log all your activity in the form of metadata or even content if they have the storage capacity, and keep those logs on hand for years. Remember, storage is cheap! In this case, if the VPN itself has been subverted, it is no better than connecting to TOR through an ISP. Another thing to mention to those who will use VPNs regardless of whether you are using TOR at the time, be aware of when you are and are not connected to your VPN. Sometimes VPNs can unexpectedly drop connections, and you may not even be aware of it. If the main reason you are using a VPN is to hide TOR usage from your ISP, then if your VPN drops, your ISP will start seeing your TOR traffic without the VPN encryption.

There is a greater, hidden risk involved as well. You could refer to it as user error or a temporary failure of the security mindset. What if, just once, you forget that you are connected to your VPN and punch in your address on Google Maps to find directions somewhere, or worse, log into your webmail account? Well, guess what Google does with all data entered into their system; they keep it, and they likely keep it indefinitely. Storage is cheap! So, if one day, the NSA identifies you on the TOR network through whatever means, there is already an evidentiary link to your VPN IP address as well as your physical location. Remember what we said about shared credentials (identities) being weak? Your IP address and VPN membership are also types of identities.

At this point, investigators might ask the VPN to turn over data on their users. The investigation might have nothing to do with any actual crime – the object might simply be to identify TOR users, a project which the NSA is indeed pursuing. If the VPN refuses to comply because they are not subject to US law, or for whatever reason, LE may check some of the big surveillance websites out there to see if you slipped up and used that IP address for anything else online. They will check logs from Google, Yahoo, Facebook, Twitter, Netflix, and other big data collection companies to see who has been using that IP address to connect to their servers.

If you accidentally punched in your address on Google when connected to that VPN, you are now a suspect. So, security mindset! Just because your IP address is masked by a VPN does not mean you are untraceable if you make a mistake. One of the benefits of TOR in this regard is that you get a new identity every time you connect. This may or may not be the case with your VPN, so please check and make sure.

Lastly, a word on how to connect to TOR over a VPN. If you are using Open VPN like I recommended, then it is really quite simple.

Make sure you are connected to your VPN by checking your IP address on any website, such as **WhatIsMyIpAddress.com** to make sure it has changed. Then, open TOR or open TAILS and start using TOR, and you are now connected to TOR over a VPN.

Using TOR to Connect to a VPN

Next, let's talk about the advantages and disadvantages of using TOR to connect to a VPN. This would look something like:

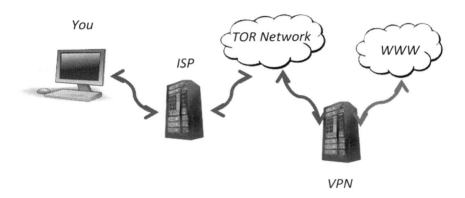

Note: All the communication links before the VPN server are red (encrypted), but be aware that there are different crypto protocols operating on different links.

The chief benefit of doing this is as follows: you are anonymous to your VPN just in case they keep logs. Should you do something you are not supposed to using the VPN and a website or server grabs your VPN IP address, even if the VPN manages to keep logs of everything you do, they can only identify you as an anonymous TOR user. This applies as long as you did not, like an idiot, pay the VPN using your credit card or PayPal account. If you use Bitcoin and took reasonable precautions to obscure the Bitcoin trail, you will have nothing to worry about. As an additional bonus, some websites block

TOR users from connecting to their websites or servers. For instance, Wikipedia does not allow articles to be edited by recognizable TOR users since the anonymity may make some people irresponsible. By using your VPN in the way sketched above, "your" IP address is that of the VPN server rather than the TOR exit node, likely bypassing their filters.

Yet, another advantage is that if your VPN connection does drop (and they do!), this will only reveal your TOR IP address instead of your real IP address. And finally, if you are passing through a compromised (taken over by hackers or spies) TOR exit node, your information will remain encrypted through the VPN's encryption protocol. This is a good thing if you are passing through a compromised exit node, but do not forget that the VPN could be logging everything you are doing anyway. **Do not trust anybody who has access to your unencrypted data!**

Of course, doing things this way means that your ISP will know that you are using TOR, when, and for how long. This may or may not matter to you, but it is something I need to mention. Secondly, you will be unable to visit hidden services websites. Remember those .onion sites we talked about in the beginning? You need to be connected to the TOR network to visit those hidden service websites, and you can't loop back into TOR using the VPN.

"But I am connected to TOR, aren't I?" you ask. Yes, you are, but your final interface to the internet is *not* part of the TOR network, it comes from your VPN, and your VPN is likely not configured for TOR. For you to be able to connect to a hidden service, you must either be connected directly to TOR or use a VPN to connect to TOR. TOR must be your final node of connectivity to visit onion websites.

The choice is ultimately up to you, now that you have a better idea of the tradeoffs involved. Every individual in their own circumstances will have different reasons for wanting to do VPN to TOR or TOR to VPN, or just TOR, or only VPN. Whatever choice you make, please keep all the things we've covered about the subject in mind. Remember especially that none of these techniques will save you if you enter anything identifiable about yourself online. Do not log into your Facebook account using your VPN. Do not check your email or search a nearby address on Google using your VPN. In fact, stay away from Google altogether unless absolutely necessary.

There are two other search engines out now that do not store information about their users.

#1 – DuckDuckGo. They have both a clearnet URL and a hidden services URL for both types of users.

https://www.duckduckgo.com

http://3g2upl4pq6kufc4m.onion/ – Please note the hidden services mirror is not HTTPS but is **.onion**.

#2 – StartPage. This server also does not store any information about its users.

https://www.startpage.com

How to do it: After a long search, I have found a way you can connect TOR -> VPN. It is not perfect, and some might not agree with the way I managed it, but it works, and I am giving it to you as an option. Unfortunately, it only works for Windows users at this time.

If you look back at the information above regarding combining VPN and TOR, then you will find some reasons why you might want to do so, and some of us might not have found a compelling reason to do it. However, I was unable to provide you with a way to connect to a VPN using TOR so that the VPN does not know who you are. When it comes to TOR -> VPN, if you cannot trust your VPN, which you should do no more than you trust any online service, then keeping your IP identity hidden from your VPN is a good idea. Also, with more and more people using TOR, but with only around 4000 TOR exit nodes, many of the exit node IP addresses are being flagged as spammers on popular websites, thus limiting the ability of well-meaning TOR users to post on message boards, such as Stack Exchange.

In any case, the way that I found you can implement TOR -> VPN is by using a virtual machine, let's say Virtual Box, running another instance of Windows. You also want to run TOR Expert and

Tortilla on your host OS. Their respective online tutorials should be enough to set you up. Next, set your Virtual Box to route all its network traffic through Tortilla (bridge adapter), which in turn routes it all through TOR. Currently, Tortilla is only supported by Windows, which is why this option is only available to Windows users at this time. Doing this also makes it easier to do things securely, like watching videos on YouTube.

Now that you have your Windows Virtual Machine accessing the internet via TOR, you can install a VPN of your choice, preferably one using OpenVPN, on your Windows Guest OS and connect to it. Check your IP address using one of the many websites offering this service before and after connecting; you should see different IP addresses. If all went well, you now have a virtual machine running TOR -> VPN. Then, if you want to add another layer, you can load TOR browser bundle onto your virtual machine and run that as well, giving you TOR -> VPN -> TOR for another layer of security. Also, you have the option using this method to use a VPN on your host OS, then TOR Expert with Tortilla, then another VPN on your guest OS, then TOR browser, giving you VPN -> TOR -> VPN -> TOR. Arguably, it gets a little ridiculous at this point.

I am not advocating any specific method; you will have to make that decision on your own. I am just giving you the knowledge necessary to make an informed decision, and you can ultimately choose which method you feel best about. For many tasks, implementing TOR -> VPN is necessary because of IP address-based usage restrictions mentioned above, and sometimes having TOR as your last node to the internet is necessary (like when accessing the onion network). Your choice!

I also know that the computer security community, in general, is trying to get away from using Windows, because of its many security vulnerabilities as well as other reasons.However, if you have no other way of staying anonymous from your VPN than this, then I think it is a reasonable solution until we have something like Tortilla that is compatible with Linux distributions.

How to Connect to TOR on top of TOR

Whether this has any merit as an additional security measure is debatable, but at least I had fun figuring it out, so I thought I would throw it in for you anyway.

I discovered this while trying to come up with an effective way to do a TOR -> VPN connection. You can do TOR -> TOR connection with Tails by using **Tortilla again**, thus adding another layer for your adversaries to crack. Whether or not this is worth it, it is difficult to answer definitively, but I feel you should have the option. This, however, currently only works for those using Windows, because there is currently no Linux or Mac version of Tortilla. Please note as well that this will noticeably slow down your connection since you are going through TOR twice. Here is the official homepage of Tortilla:

https://github.com/CrowdStrike/Tortilla

And the official download page for the prebuilt standalone exe below. There is a link to it on the homepage if you do not trust me (and you shouldn't!).

http://www.crowdstrike.com/community-tools/

The actual implementation is in fact quite easy. You need to first download **TOR Expert Bundle** from the TOR Project download page and install it on your computer, or better yet, your USB drive.

https://www.torproject.org/download/download.html.en

Next, open the **tor.exe** and let it run until it says **Bootstrapped 100% Done**. Next, you will want to run the tortilla.exe file (make sure you run it with Administrator privileges). Also, if you are running Windows Vista or later, you will likely get an error that this program does not have a valid certificate because it is actually signed with something called a test-signed certificate. In this case, you need to allow test-signed drivers to run on your computer.

To do this, simply go to your Start Menu and type in the search box "command." When the text-based command prompt starts, you right-clickit and click Run as Administrator, and it will open up a command prompt. Next, type in the following command: **Bcdedit.exe -set TESTSIGNING ON** and this will allow Windows to install test-signed drivers. Restart your computer, and you will see in the bottom right-hand corner after you restart **Test Mode Windows**. Now you can run Tortilla and let it connect to TOR. Remember to have **tor.exe** from TOR Expert Bundle open first.

Finally, you open up Virtual Box (or whatever Virtual Machine software you are using) and click **Settings** on the Tails virtual machine. Click on the **Network** tab and change the drop-down menu where it says **Attached to**: to **Bridged Adapter** and in the drop-down menu below it, called **Name:** Select **Tortilla Adapter**. Now your Virtual Machine, in this case, Tails, will always connect to the internet **through Tortilla**, which connects through TOR. And since Tails establishes its own connection to TOR, you will be running TOR over top of TOR.

If you are interested in learning more about the creator of Tortilla, he did a presentation at the 2013 Black Hat USA conference. Feel free to watch his talk at the YouTube link below. But, again, keep your security mindset in view. YouTube is owned by Google, and there are not many hits on this video so any snooping party might correlate users who watch that video with users from forums and the deep web. Make sure you do not watch the video on YouTube with your real IP address. At the very least use a VPN or find another site that has it hosted. Always be extra paranoid.

https://youtu.be/G_jDPQU-8YQ

Tips for Tails

So far, we've managed to boot the Tails operating system from an SD card or USB drive, run the OpenPGP application, edited text documents, and used the browser. This operating system is capable of more than just that, though, so let's see what else we can do with it.

Disk Encryption

Another very useful security feature is called Whole Disk

Encryption or Full Disk Encryption. From here on, I will refer to it as FDE (Full Disk Encryption). Tails comes with an FDE feature already incorporated, which is another reason why I like this operating system from a security viewpoint. It has many of these useful functions for your protection. Essentially, FDE will protect your drive, whether SD or USB, from the people who may just come for you one day. The way in which it does this is that it formats your drive and rewrites the file system in an encrypted format so that it can only be accessed by someone who has the passphrase.

If you lose your passphrase, just like in PGP, no recovery is possible. Your only choice is to format the drive and start over again, minus whatever data you've lost. So, make sure you remember it! And please, for the love of God, Allah, Buddha, etc… don't store the passphrase on your hard drive somewhere. The tutorial on how to do this is located at the following webpage.

https://tails.boum.org/doc/encryption_and_privacy/encrypted_volumes/index.en.html

File Shredding

As mentioned before, when you delete a file from a disk, you're actually just removing the address for that file. The data stays right where it is unless you use a special utility.

If there is any chance that "they" might come knocking someday, or in fact, if you store sensitive data of any kind on your computer and theft is remotely possible, the first step to protecting your data is to encrypt everything. Use PGP when communicating with others and always shred your files when finished with them.

Even using freeware file recovery tools, you can recover virtually any file that has been recently removed. File shredding prevents this by overwriting random data to the relevant location instead. The idea is that instead of erasing the file's location, you scramble the remaining data until it becomes unrecoverable.

There are different viewpoints on whether you can just overwrite a file once, or if you need to do it multiple times to ensure secrecy. Supposedly, the NSA recommends 3 times, supposedly, the

Department of Defense recommends 7 times, and an old paper by a man named Peter Gutmann, written in the 90's, recommended 35 times. For all the practical purposes, I'm sure between 3-7 times is sufficient, and several people out there believe 1 time will get the job done.

The reasoning behind this is that some people believe the magnetic or solid-state bits of the drive may retain some trace of the original data even after being overwritten several times, so to ensure randomness, you should do multiple passes. Do whatever you feel most comfortable with, but I really think 3 passes is sufficient, although it can't hurt, every now and then, to run 7 passes and just leave it running overnight.

You will normally want to access the programs that can do file shredding from Windows or whatever operating system your computer is running. In addition to shredding, such applications can typically erase your files from your Recycling Bin, delete your temporary internet files and even wipe your free disk space to make sure everything gets cleaned up. As part of the security mindset, you occasionally need to wonder: did I have any sensitive material on my hard drive? If so, maybe I need to shred my free disk space. When emptying your Recycle Bin, you should always use a shredder. When deleting less than1 GB at a time, you can easily do 7 passes pretty quickly.

To put the value of these utilities into perspective, the leader of a hacking group called LulzSec, called Topiary, has been banned, as part of his sentence, from using any type of file shredding applications. In this way, if the FBI wants to check up on him, they can. File shredding keeps your deleted files actually deleted.

Here are some file shredding applications you can use.

http://www.dban.org/
http://www.fileshredder.org/
https://www.piriform.com/ccleaner

Password Management

As mentioned before, it is basic security mindset to use different logins and passwords for different services. It is also humanly impossible to keep track of upwards of a dozen unique, unidentifiable and secure credentials without writing them down, which is a serious risk all by itself.

Well, Tails has another very useful program called KeePassX. When you have multiple logins, it is hard to keep track of them all, so it's reasonable to store them all in a single file that is strongly encrypted. KeePassX is a good utility for this.

https://tails.boum.org/doc/encryption_and_privacy /manage_passwords/index.en.html

You never want to use nicknames or locations, or anything else that is related to yourself, when you post or create usernames online. Another precaution you might need to take is to break existing, identifiable patterns. If you frequently misspell the same words or post similar comments on different message boards, this can be used to identify you. Always proofread anything you post publicly, or even privately because the feds will always attempt to connect seemingly innocuous things to you and your online identity.

Even think about when you use your computer. If you are logged on from home every day from seven to eight in the morning, and again after eight at night, monitoring can at least figure out your time zone and probably much besides. Do you have other predictable patterns that you could break once in a while? It's worth it to think about these things when you post online.

Expect that every single word you type online is being read by the feds. To them, this is much easier than tracking drug lords on the streets. They sit in an office and read forum posts and speculate. Don't underestimate the resources at their disposal. Always treat everything as compromised, always treat everybody as compromisable, and don't ever think anybody will ever go to prison on your behalf. If somebody can avoid 10 or 20 years behind bars by informing on you, they will do it in a second.

The perfect example is Sabu from LulzSec. After he was busted and facing 112 years in jail, they allowed him to make a deal to assist in the capture of his friends, and he ended up getting many of his former comrades arrested. Even people who are otherwise loyal will turn their backs on you when it comes down to their freedom.

Removing Metadata from Files

Unless you've spent considerable time recently living in a cave, you will have heard the word "metadata." Put simply, metadata is data attached to a message that doesn't form part of the message itself. This may include, for instance, a timestamp or addressing information.

Now, the security mindset should be gently tinkling alarm bells at this thought. Data piggybacking on your data, which you didn't know was there? Not ideal. There is a bit of a famous story about an online hacker named w0rmer that would take pictures of his girlfriend and post them online after he would deface a webpage. What he either forgot or didn't know was that photos taken with the iPhone and other smartphones save the GPS coordinates of where the picture was taken and store it in the metadata of the picture. Check out this article below.

https://encyclopediadramatica.es/W0rmer

You need to remove this metadata! Otherwise, you could end up in federal prison with w0rmer. Luckily, Tails has a solution for this! See why I love Tails?

Applications -> Accessories -> Metadata Anonymization Toolkit

Please get a clearer idea of how this works by reading the following page.

https://mat.boum.org/

Please note the currently supported formats, which in terms of pictures are only jpg, jpeg, and png. Unfortunately, MAT is not perfect, and I wouldn't solely rely on it so a better idea would be not to upload images of yourself or your family online, especially bragging about a hack you committed. Please read the site provided above for more information.

While we are on the subject of metadata, when it comes to photos, there is another risk involved called EXIF data, which is another kind of metadata specifically related to images and may not be properly removed by the Tails utility MAT.

EXIF data stands for **Exchangeable Image File**

format and affects JPG, JPEF, TIF and WAV files. A photo taken with a GPS-enabled camera will record where and when it was taken, as well as the unique ID number of the device. This is all done by default, often without the buyer being told.

In December 2012, anti-virus programmer John McAfee was arrested in Guatemala while fleeing from alleged persecution in neighboring Belize. This, incidentally, is a fairly good example of someone being badgered by police without much actual evidence against them. Vice magazine published an exclusive interview with McAfee "on the run" that included a photo of McAfee with a Vice reporter. Unfortunately, it had been taken with a phone that included the latitude and longitude. This metadata allowed LE to locate McAfee in Guatemala, where he was captured two days later.

Convert your photos into PNG-format to strip away the EXIF data. To check if your photo has any revealing EXIF data attached to it, I would advise consulting:

http://www.viewexifdata.com/

Alternatively, you can conduct a quick search online for apps that can identify and display metadata contained in your photos before you upload them. Be very careful with any files that you upload online, because you never know what type of harmful data these files could be hiding. It helps to use Tails, but always consider everything you put online as a potential piece of evidence to be used against you and always prepare for the day the feds come to your door.

Verifying Downloaded Installation Files

As a general rule of thumb, you should **always** download files from the homepages of their respective developers.

TOR: https://www.torproject.org
Tails: https://www.tails.boum.org
Virtual Box: https://www.virtualbox.org/

Why is this important? There are people who host malware-infected versions of these programs and will build legitimate looking sites to try and get you to download their version, which can install things like backdoors into your computers, key loggers, and all types of nasty surprises. Sometimes, developers will offer mirrors for their projects, which are simply just alternative locations to download from to relieve some of the burden on the primary server. Sometimes, these mirrors can get hacked without the developers being any the wiser. Incidentally, this is also a good reason not to use pirated software but pay for the unadulterated original and any patches that may become available. Security mindset demands, at the very least, that you don't actively infect your own computer with spyware!

Still, at times, the official webpage might not be available. Maybe you do not have TOR or Tails on your laptop while traveling abroad, and the hotel that you are staying at has TOR's homepage blocked. There are times when you may need to find an alternative mirror to download certain things. Then, of course, there is the infamous **man-in-the-middle** attack where an attacker can inject malicious code into your network traffic and alter the file you are downloading, even while the download is in progress. The TOR developers have even reported that attackers have the capability of tricking your browser into thinking you are visiting the TOR homepage when, in fact, you are not.

So, what do you do about it? Fortunately, there is an easy countermeasure to verify that the file you downloaded is, in fact, legitimate. The best tool for this is **GnuPG**. The TOR developers recommend you get it from the following page (Windows Users).

http://www.gpg4win.org/download.html

You can install this program on your USB drive or on your host operating system (your actual computer's operation system, as opposed to the one run in Virtual Box, is referred to as your Host OS). So, download it, run it, install it, and we will start showing you how to use GnuPG.

If you remain on the GnuPG download page, you will see something under the big green box that is called **OpenPGP signature**. Download that into the same folder as the GnuPG file — this is the file that the download was signed with. Basically, it is the developer's signature saying, 'I created this file' (authentication using an asymmetric protocol, in technical terms). You will also need a

PGP public key to verify this signature. So, to sum it up so far, the signature is created using the PGP private key and can be verified by the PGP public key. The signature file is used to verify the program itself. So, let us grab the PGP public key for GnuPG as well.

If you look on the same download page, under the heading Installation, you will see a link where it says **Verify the integrity of the file**. It will lead you to the following page.

http://gpg4win.org/package-integrity.html

Note the following statement: **The signatures have been created with the following OpenPGP certificate Intevation File Distribution Key (Key ID: EC70B1B8)**. This is the link to the page that hosts the PGP public key file that you need to download, so let's go there. On the page, we just navigated to, go to the bottom right where it says **Intevation-Distribution-Key (public OpenPGPkey for signing files)** and download that file. This is the PGP public key file. Save it to the same place as your signature file for ease of use.

Okay, now that we have both the signature file and the PGP public key, let us now verify our download. The first thing you need to do is navigate to the PGP public key file, called **Intervation-Distribution-Key.asc**, right-click it and go to **More GpgEX Options** and down to **Import Keys**. This will import the PGP public key into your keyring, and now you can verify the file with the signature.

Right-click the installation file you want to verify, in this case, **gpg4win-2.2.1.exe,** and go to **More GpgEX Options** and scroll to **Verify**. It should automatically have the name of the signature file under Input File, but if it does not, navigate to the signature file and make sure the box below it where it says **Input file is a detached signature** is checked. Look at the bottom and click Decrypt/Verify, and you will likely get the following message:

Not enough information to check signature validity. Check details.

That sucks. Things were going so well for us! Actually, this is completely fine. Click on **Show Details**, you are looking for something in particular.

Signed on 2013-10-07 08:31 by distribution-key@intervation.de (Key ID: 0xEC70B1B8). The validity of the signature cannot be verified.

If you navigate back to the page from Gpg4Win that says **Check Integrity** where you found the link to the page that contained the PGP public key, you will see on that page:

Intevation File Distribution Key (Key ID: EC70B1B8)

Note the key ID from your decrypt result and the key ID from the Check Integrity page and note the email address ending in the same URL that we downloaded the PGP public key from. We have a match! I will explain the reason for this warning message later.

Now, that we verified that our verification program is the real deal, let's try and verify our Tails ISO file, since if we have a compromised Tails OS, then nothing we do on top of it will be secure. Let us get right to the Tails download page.

https://tails.boum.org/download/index.en.html

Scroll down to where it says **Tails 0.22 signature** and download that to your Tails folder, where you've saved the ISO file that we've downloaded previously. Next, scroll down to where it says **Tails signing key**, which will be our PGP public key. Do exactly as you did before: import the key, then click Verify, and specify the signature file (if it has not already been automatically selected), use the same settings, and you will get the same warning message. As explained by Tails,

"If you see the following warning:
Not enough information to check the signature validity.
Signed on ... by tails@boum.org (Key ID: 0xBE2CD9C1
The validity of the signature cannot be verified.

Then the ISO image is still correct, and valid according to the Tails signing key that you downloaded. This warning is related to the

trust that you put in the Tails signing key. See, Trusting Tails signing key. To remove this warning, you would have to personally sign the Tails signing key with your own key."

In other words, you need to basically promise that the PGP public key you downloaded is safe by signing the PGP public key with your own private key. If you do not fully understand the implications of this transfer of trust, don't worry. We do not really need to do that, and I will not be presenting a tutorial on how. Tails suggests that if you are worried about a compromised PGP public key, just download the key from multiple sources and compare them. If they all match, you can pretty much be sure that you are using a genuine PGP key. Now, let us finally move on to TOR, because this one will be a little less straightforward. However, once you do this one, you should be able to figure out how to verify anything. Navigate to their download page and find the package that you want.

https://www.torproject.org/download/download.html.en

To keep things simple, let us choose Tor Browser Bundle 3.5 (assuming this is the version you installed), and under the orange box, you will see a link **(sig)**. This is the link for the signature file, and by now you should know what to do with it. Next, we need the PGP public key, right? Well, it turns out that with so many developers working on TOR, there are multiple PGP public keys, and various bundles were signed with various distinct keys. So, we need to find the PGP public key that belongs to our Tor Browser Bundle specifically. Check out this page.

https://www.torproject.org/docs/signing-keys.html.en

It has a list of all the signing keys used by them, and you can certainly use these key IDs to get what you need by simply right-clicking on the signature file and click verify. You will get a warning: **Not enough information to check signature validity. Show Details.**

And in details, it will say the following warning:

Signed on 2013-12-19 08:34 with unknown certificate 0x416F061063FEE659

Do make a note of this code, which is called a *Fingerprint*. For the moment, let's just check the last eight characters, **0x63FEE659** (the 0x-prefix means it's a hexadecimal number, using 0 to 9 as well as A to F to write numbers up to 15 in a single digit). They are exactly the same as the key ID of Erinn Clark, who signs the TOR Browser Bundles. This is a fairly good check and may be sufficient in a lot of cases, but let's see how we can be more thorough.

If you haven't already, download the program called **Kleopatra** and install it to Windows. Once installed, open the application and go to **Open Certificate Manager**. A certificate is a form of credential, like your username and password, but for the authenticity of servers, files or software, and it uses public-private key encryption. We are going to import the full keys using this manager. For future reference, on the tab labeled **Other Certificates,** you will find the Tails and Intevation (GnuPG) keys we used earlier stored for when you need to download a new version of those programs and verify them once more.

We are going to be following the instructions from the **verifying signatures** page on the TOR Project website. It might be a good idea to read their instructions in tandem with this section.

https://www.torproject.org/docs/verifying-signatures.html.en

We need to define an online directory from where keys will be imported. For now, let's set this value to where the PGP public keys are stored as we saw on the TOR website. Click **Settings** followed by **Configure Kleopatra**. Next, click **New** and enter the following URL, which you can also find on the page above, **pool.sks-keyservers.net**, then leave all other fields in their default state and click OK.

Now, we're ready to go. Click the button that says **Lookup Certificates On Server** in order to search for Errin Clark's PGP public key by searching for her **fingerprint** provided on the TOR webpage at the URL above. The fingerprint we are entering is **0x416F061063FEE659**, and doesn't it seem like you've seen part of it before? It should, it is the number we got back the first time we tried verifying the TOR browser bundle, which we did without the actual PGP public key. You can probably ignore any warnings that turn up while searching; just click OK, and you should see Errin Clark's key. Select this and click **Import**. You should now have her key listed under **Imported Certificates** in Kleopatra.

Now, let us go back and verify that program signature one more time and see what happens. You should get something like the following:

Not enough information to check signature validity. Signed on 201-12-17 12:41 by errin@torproject.org (Key ID: 0x63FEE659). The validity of the signature cannot be verified.

TOR also explains this warning message in their words, in case you are still concerned about the warning message:

"Notice that there is a warning because you haven't assigned a trust index to this person. This means that GnuPG verified that the key made that signature, but it's up to you to decide if that key really belongs to the developer. The best method is to meet the developer in person and exchange key fingerprints."

I do not know about you, but I am content with the validity of the downloaded files, and I have no desire to hunt up Erinn Clark just to get her key fingerprint! Getting this information through an official website is good enough 99% of the time. We've already proved that our browser is the genuine article, free from any form of fiddling or malware. Now that you know what to do when the PGP public key file is not directly hosted on the site itself, you have no more excuses not to verify your downloads.

TOR Chat Secure Messaging

By now, you should have grasped that sending unencrypted information over the internet is nearly as insecure as publishing it in your local newspaper. This applies to email (and webmail in particular), instant messaging, Skype, whatever. Even if the message content is not stored, the metadata – origin and destination address, message size, date, etc. – is almost certainly recorded and monitored. Should LE ever become interested in you, they could potentially have a record of everything you said online and everybody you had contact with for the past decade – a scary thought.

The only solution, apart from disconnecting your phone and learning to hunt with a bow and arrow, is a suitable security mindset. Always assume anything you do not encrypt is visible to whoever can do the most damage with it. Luckily for us, we do now have some tools in the box to enhance our online security and privacy: PGP encryption for files and messages, TOR and VPNs to disguise your IP address (and therefore your identity), accessing TOR's hidden services or at least using https, and most importantly, *thinking about what you are doing* and knowing enough to make informed decisions. The discussion would be incomplete without referencing one more very convenient tool, called TorChat.

Many people use the instant messaging services provided by their webmail, Facebook or what have you; TorChat is the secure version. The nature of its architecture is decentralized (meaning no single failure point for any would-be Big Brother to exploit) and uses TOR hidden services as a logical network. To put it another way, it communicates over the TOR network using the .onion URL protocol, providing that all-important end-to-end encryption for users.

It can be used for ordinary text messaging or secure file transmission. Take a moment to ponder the difference between sending your company's payroll data to an accountant using a) email, or b) an encrypted service. In the case of "a," you are practically handing out flyers containing the name, address, salary, bank account, social security number, and tax information of every employee! If you still think this does not leave you and them extremely vulnerable, you haven't been paying attention to either this book or the news for a while now.

You don't even have to run it through Tails; in fact, they don't seem to be compatible. TorChat applications are currently available for Windows, Linux, and smartphones. A beta version (an unproven, untested program) is available for Mac users, but like any pre-release software, it should not be regarded as 100% reliable. For whatever smartphone you have, look for TorChat in either the Apple Store or Android Market, and tell your friends about the inherent benefits of secure instant messaging.

How you will use it in practice is that you will receive a unique ID code 16 characters long, which is randomly created by TOR when the client software on your phone or PC is run the first time. You can think of it as being the .onion address of a hidden service. If you send a message, it bounces through the TOR network until it reaches your recipient's hidden service. For example, the first time you open TorChat, your computer might generate **d0dj309jfj94jfgf.onion** and from here on out, **d0dj309jfj94jfgf** you shall be named. This will be like your secret phone number you can share with people that you want to be able to message you. Here is the homepage of TorChat:

https://github.com/prof7bit/TorChat
http://www.sourcemac.com/?page=torchat

MAC users

Using the application is pretty intuitive using whatever operating system you have installed; once you run it the first time, everything is set up for you without having to lift a finger. When the picture beside your TorChat ID turns green, you are online and can start pinging your contacts. Right-click and choose **Add Contact** to enter any TorChat IDs you've been given.

Like with most software, there's a healthy debate going on as to whether or not TorChat is completely secure. The general opinion is that TorChat, being essentially a chunk of software to use the TOR protocol, is about as safe as TOR itself. Still, it pays to be mindful that any system can be hacked, so keep up the good habits we've already discussed: don't send personal information without good reason, PGP-encrypt when appropriate, etc.

Here is another article that goes into a little bit more detail on how TorChat works. You can access it over the onion network.

http://kpvz7ki2v5agwt35.onion/wiki/index.php/
Hacking_TorChat

PART THREE: DEEPER INTO THE WEB

Hiding TOR from your ISP: Bridges and Pluggable Transports

When you connect to the deep web using TOR, your ISP or VPN cannot read your messages, but they can indeed see that you are using TOR. Now, bear in mind that using TOR is in no way illegal, but LE might decide that it is suspicious. It could be argued that both your ISP and your VPN have a legal and ethical obligation to protect your privacy, for instance by not keeping logs of your connection. LE tends to disagree and is quite willing to exert pressure on either. Those who rely on VPNs and ISPs are historically known to end up in jail.

We've already looked at the implications of accessing TOR over a VPN, or a VPN over TOR, and indeed TOR over TOR. I've tried to present the facts in an open and honest manner, and you are hopefully now capable of making decisions regarding your own protection. The only point I wish to reiterate is that you should not place undue trust in people you don't know well, and this includes your ISP.

Luckily, there are other options you can use to hide your TOR traffic from your ISP, called *Bridges*, and several different flavors of *pluggable transports*. They are also useful if you live in a country with heavy internet censorship, such as prohibiting the use of TOR altogether.

Now, we, who live in the real world, know that, for example, investigative journalists and pacifist activists are often monitored, and usually with the active cooperation of their ISP. It might be prudent to sidestep any monitoring from the get-go by using alternative entry points to the TOR network. These are called Bridges (or Bridge Relays). In essence, all of their addresses are not publicized. Your ISP might still be able to detect that you are using TOR, but the likelihood is reduced.

Let's take a look at the following:

https://tails.boum.org/doc/first_steps/startup_optio ns/bridge_mode/index.en.html

We need to find the location of some Bridges first, which will be done using Tails the way we've already configured it. Once Tails is set up to use Bridges, we won't be able to access TOR without the addresses of functioning Bridges:

https://bridges.torproject.org/bridges

Prove that you are a living person and not a web-crawling robot, and you should get a list of Bridges like the following, actual list:

"5.20.130.121:9001 63dd98cd106a95f707efe538e98e7a6f92d28f94 106.186.19.58:443 649027f9ea9a8e11578742543046386e14e0ffa 69.125.172.116:443 43c3a8e5594d8e62799e96dc137d695ae4bd24b2"

Of course, anyone, who wishes to, can see these addresses, so they might be known to anybody who is really interested in what strangers do online, but they are a good place to begin. Alternatively, send an email to **bridges@bridges.torproject.org** with "get bridges" in the body (without the quotes). This only works from a Gmail or Yahoo account, which, for security purposes, should be set up using TOR. You should be receiving a list of about three Bridges shortly; save them to a USB drive or write them down if you have the patience.

Now we have what we need to configure Tails for bridge mode. In order to do this, we have to add the **Bridge** boot option to the boot menu, which is the first screen to be displayed when Tails starts up. When you see the black screen saying "Boot Tails" with the options (1) Live and (2) Live (Fail Safe), press Tab, and you'll be presented with some other options at the bottom of the screen. To add the bridge option, add a space and enter *bridge* followed by pressing enter. Tails is now entering bridge mode.

Once Tails is running, you will see a notice that you're working in bridge mode and shouldn't play around with the default IP address,127.0.0.1:*. Since the computer asked us nicely, we'll leave that just as it is and click OK. This brings up another window, allowing us to enter the three addresses we've obtained online. For general interest, the number after the colon is a port, which is where the server will be "listening" for your connection. We'll enter:

"5.20.130.121:9001
106.186.19.58:443
69.125.172.116:443"

Click on the green plus sign after each address to add it to Tails, and on OK to accept. Take a look at the yellow onion icon in the top right corner, it should be turning green in a few seconds – you're now connected to TOR using a Bridge. What this means is, unless your ISP goes to some effort to know the IP addresses of all Bridges, they do not see you using TOR.

You may want to know a bit more about the Bridges you're using, for instance, where they are physically located, who operates them, and so forth. You can start by searching for any of the IP lookup services online and entering the Bridge's address. This shows us:

"5.20.130.121 – Country: Lithuania
106.186.19.58:443 – Country: Japan
69.125.172.116:443 – Country: New Jersey, United States"

You may choose a Bridge in your physical vicinity for slightly reduced latency, or decide to steer clear of any server located in a country with limited respect for civil rights. More importantly, it is an excellent idea to search out new Bridges, whose IP address will not be generally known. The extra level of privacy a Bridge provides relies exclusively on its address.

Based on this fact, using a Bridge on its own is not sufficient. According to Jacob Applebaum, a TOR developer, traffic routed through a Bridge can still be analyzed through a technique called DPI (deep packet inspection), revealing the protocol used for the communication (TOR, in this case). Most internet censorship relies on having an up-to-date list of "bad" servers or TOR entry nodes, but, if the government is willing to spend the resources (think Iran or China), they can still block access to TOR.

"Lately, censors have found ways to block TOR even when clients are using Bridges. They usually do this by installing boxes in ISPs that peek at network traffic and detect TOR; when TOR is detected, they block the traffic flow.

To circumvent such sophisticated censorship, TOR *introduced obfuscated Bridges.* **These Bridges use special plugins called pluggable transports, which obfuscate the traffic flow of TOR, making its detection harder."**

https://www.torproject.org/docs/bridges#Pluggabl eTransports

As mentioned in the quote above, pluggable transports help to fool your ISP, the Great Firewall, and other kinds of censors. It does this by making your TOR traffic look innocuous and random. At the moment, the most popular type of pluggable transports is called Obfuscated Bridges, which run one of the following two protocols:

1. obfs2
2. obfs3

Obfs2 (The Two Obfuscator) is described in detail on the following official page:

https://gitweb.torproject.org/pluggable-transports/obfsproxy.git/blob/HEAD:/doc/obfs2/obfs 2-protocol-spec.txt

Essentially, obfs defeats DPI by making your network traffic look like random data packets instead of TOR. However, you should know that, should a hacker be able to "sniff" your network connection while you first connect to the Obfuscated Bridge, there is a chance that cryptographic data can be stolen in this way. The actual contents of the data you send and receive will still be protected by the TOR protocol, but it will once again be possible to discover that you are using TOR. Such an attack, requiring some skill and resources, is not the most likely threat, but the security mindset demands that you are at least aware of the possibility.

To learn more about Obfs3 (The Three Obfuscator), have a look at:

https://gitweb.torproject.org/pluggable-transports/obfsproxy.git/blob/HEAD:/doc/obfs3/obfs3-protocol-spec.txt

Obfs3 is technically quite similar to obfs2, with the main difference being that the initial handshake between your computer and the Obfuscated Bridge is more secure than obfs2 (a customized Diffie-Hellman key exchange, in case you like big words).

So, onto implementing this in Tails. You may have to expend some effort to get them, using a Gmail or Yahoo account over TOR. Send an email to bridges@bridges.torproject.org with the body as "transport obfs2" or "transport obfs3" without the quotes. Because these addresses are somewhat confidential, you can only submit one email per three-hour period. Once you get a reply, enter them into Tails as follows:

obfs3 83.212.101.2:42782
obfs2 70.182.182.109:54542

TOR also lists a few Obfuscated Bridges on their homepage, such as the following:

obfs3 83.212.101.2:42782
obfs3 83.212.101.2:443
obfs3 169.229.59.74:31493
obfs3 169.229.59.75:46328
obfs3 209.141.36.236:45496
obfs3 208.79.90.242:35658
obfs3 109.105.109.163:38980

obfs3 109.105.109.163:47779
obfs2 83.212.100.216:47870
obfs2 83.212.96.182:46602
obfs2 70.182.182.109:54542
obfs2 128.31.0.34:1051
obfs2 83.212.101.2:45235

If a line does not start with either obfs2 or obfs3, that is the address for an ordinary, non-Obfuscated Bridge. At times, there may not be any Obfuscated Bridges available, so just try again in a few days. Hosting these Bridges costs money, and at any given time there may only be a few hundred available, with only about 40 running obfs3. So, even though it offers good security, there exists an architectural bottleneck.

If you want to help ameliorate this shortage, you could consider running your own Obfuscated Bridge. How to go about it is beyond the scope of personal information security, but the following page will get you going in the right direction:

https://www.whonix.org/wiki/Hosting_a_(private)_(ob fuscated)_bridge_or_(exit)_relay

What you will be doing is renting a VPS (Virtual Private Server) and setting it up as an obfs2 or obfs3 proxy. Depending on your situation, you can set it up to be a private Obfuscated Bridge, the address of which is not given out to other users. In any case, do not forget that a rented VPS is only as secure as the owner wants it to be.

Apart from Obfuscated Bridges, an exciting new development in terms of pluggable transport is called a **Flash Proxy.** This is still a little way from being a completely developed protocol, so it is better to wait until its security and functionality have been thoroughly tested. The "flash" part implies more or less what you think it should, something brief and transient. The notion is that, since internet censors use IP addresses to block traffic, these IP addresses should be changed faster than these digital monitors can track them. Essentially, Flash Proxy means using a non-obfuscated Bridge so that your ISP and LE will not know that you are using TOR. If somebody is going to the trouble of using DPI (deep packet inspection), TOR use can still be detected.

The major benefit of Flash Proxies is that they can be run by many people all at once. They might be created when some internet user visits a website equipped with a specific plugin that temporarily turns their browser into a proxy, which bridges or relays your messages to the TOR network (for however long or short time they choose to be connected). In practice, you will only be using one connection actively at any given moment, but with about 5 spare connections to other proxies, in case the one you are using drops off. Here is a sample of a clear explanation:

"In addition to the TOR client and relay, we provide three new pieces. The TOR client contacts the facilitator to advertise that it needs a connection (proxy). The facilitator is responsible for keeping track of clients and proxies and assigning one to another. The flash proxy polls the facilitator for client registrations, then begins a connection to the client when it gets one. The transport plugins on the client and relay broker the connection between WebSockets and plain TCP. (Diagram below)"

https://crypto.stanford.edu/flashproxy/arch.png

A session would be established as follows:

The client (you) starts TOR and the flash proxy client (software), which enrolls your computer into the system using a secure protocol hosted by a facilitator. At this point, your computer is ready to accept a remote connection.

A remote flash proxy comes online and asks the facilitator if any requests are outstanding.

The facilitator sends information to the proxy, enabling it to connect to you.

The proxy initiates the connection to your transport plugin software.

You are now connecting to the TOR relay via the proxy.

Remembering all the ground we've covered relating to censorship or monitoring at the ISP level, the advantage of this scheme is that you are not connecting to a Bridge with a well-known IP address. You are connecting to a transitory proxy, which isn't known to be part of the TOR network. Even if a censor discovers the proxy's address within a few minutes, nothing of real value is lost – it was supposed to be temporary, and other proxies are already lined up to provide alternatives.

If you've been carefully following the explanation, you might be under the impression that the facilitator provides a single point of failure that can scupper the whole system. Not quite, the initial request for registration to the facilitator is a one-way, low-bandwidth message that might only be needed once for each session and is pretty secure. To put it another way:

"The way the client registers with the facilitator is a special rendezvous step that does not communicate directly with the facilitator, designed to be covert and very hard to block. The way this works in practice is that the flash proxy client transport plugin makes a TLS (HTTPS) connection to Gmail, and sends an encrypted email from an anonymous address (nobody@localhost) to a special facilitator registration address. The facilitator checks this mailbox periodically, decrypts the messages, and inserts the registrations they contain. The result is that anyone who can send an email to a Gmail address can do rendezvous, even if the facilitator is blocked."

https://trac.torproject.org/projects/tor/wiki/FlashProxyFAQ

You might well have another concern, namely what happens if the proxy or the facilitator has ill intentions towards you. The facilitator is chosen and operated by TOR, so there's every reason to trust its integrity. As far as the proxies are concerned, you have no way to know. But, this is the case for the whole of TOR. You can't get a specially engraved license to operate a TOR server. Any entry, exit or relay node might be compromised – but they will only see your encrypted data. The exact same thing applies to a Bridge or FlashProxy. Furthermore, if somebody wants to intercept your communication, in particular, they will have quite a time arranging that. Since anybody who visits a webpage with a particular plugin installed becomes a temporary proxy – even without knowing about it – there will be many thousands of users online at any given time. A proxy won't be able to choose what particular traffic gets routed through it.

The bad news is that this is a new technology, and Tails does not yet support it. On the other hand, you can run it directly on Windows, Linux or Apple using the Tor Pluggable Transports Tor Browser Bundle. Download it from here:

https://www.torproject.org/docs/pluggable-transports.html.en#download

Once you have it, click on the following link for a detailed, easy-to-follow guide on using it:

https://trac.torproject.org/projects/tor/wiki/FlashProxyHowto

The highlights, practically speaking, is to enable port forwarding for port 9000, add "bridge flashproxy 0.0.1.0:1" to torrc, and not change anything else unless you know what you are doing. Your firewall might prompt you to add an exception for the FlashProxy plugin; choose to do so. As long as you are using the Tor Pluggable Transports Tor Browser Bundle, you should have no difficulty.

This chapter on Bridges and pluggable transports covers quite a bit of ground, so I hope we're metaphorically still on the same page. If you like, you can start by setting Tails to use ordinary, non-obfuscated Bridges, then exploring obfs, and finally trying out Flash Proxies. Of course, until Tails supports the latter, you'll be using your computer online without the benefit of a virtual box, which is generally not recommended. In any case, try to think about the security and practical implications of your various options. Do you simply consider the fact that you use TOR to be none of your ISP's business? Is there a real risk of financial loss or legal troubles? It might make sense for you to invest the time and money into setting up a private Bridge.

If you're interested in having even more options, have a look at some pluggable transports currently in development:

"ScrambleSuit is a pluggable transport that protects against follow-up probing attacks and is also capable of changing its network fingerprint (packet length distribution, inter-arrival times, etc.). It's

part of the Obfsproxy framework. See its official page. Maintained by Philipp Winter.

http://www.cs.kau.se/philwint/scramblesuit/

Status: Undeployed

StegoTorus *is an Obfsproxy fork that extends it to a) split TOR streams across multiple connections to avoid packet size signatures and b) embed the traffic flows in traces that look like html, JavaScript, or pdf. See its git repository. Maintained by Zack Weinberg.*

https://gitweb.torproject.org/stegotorus.git

Status: Undeployed

SkypeMorph *transforms* TOR *traffic flows so they look like Skype Video. See its source code and design paper. Maintained by Ian Goldberg.*

http://crysp.uwaterloo.ca/software/SkypeMorph-0.5.1.tar.gz

http://cacr.uwaterloo.ca/techreports/2012/cacr2012-08.pdf

Status: Undeployed

Dust *aims to provide a packet-based (rather than connection-based) DPI-resistant protocol. See its git repository. Maintained by Brandon Wiley.*

https://github.com/blanu/Dust

Status: Undeployed

Format-Transforming Encryption (FTE)*transforms* TOR *traffic to arbitrary formats using their language descriptions. See the research paper and webpage.*

https://eprint.iacr.org/2012/494

https://kpdyer.com/fte/

Status: Undeployed

Also, see the unofficial pluggable transports wiki page for more pluggable transport information.

https://trac.torproject.org/projects/tor/wiki/doc/PluggableTransports"

Source:

https://www.torproject.org/docs/pluggable-transports.html.en

Your Traitor Browser: Threats in Plain Sight

We've already dealt with some fairly advanced protection software, but we would be remiss if we didn't mention some more basic vulnerabilities as well. If you've done some exploring on the TOR network, you might have realized that some functions, such as Flash video, just don't work.

Javascript is another technology used by browsers, which may open your computer to attacks. It allows a much greater range of functionality than plain http (i.e. garish websites), but at the price of potential vulnerabilities. In fact, the majority of exploits, malware, and PC takeovers happen due to Javascript code running in your browser. For instance, in mid-2013 someone in Ireland was operating a web hosting business, including hidden services and a secure email system known as Tor Mail. Unfortunately, he was arrested on charges relating to child pornography and had all his servers seized. Whether he was guilty of child abuse is not known for sure, though it did serve as a very convenient pretext for raiding his datacenter. What LE did in addition, however, was install Javascript malware on his servers to enable them to track down his customers. The following article contains more information:

https://openwatch.net/i/200/

With this example in mind, you may want to disable Javascript in your browsers when visiting any website that is not 100% trusted. A hacker may manage to insert their malicious code into a legitimate website, at which point a number of bad things can happen. You may be unexpectedly redirected to other sites, have usernames and passwords sent to the wrong server, or have a lot of information about your computer transmitted to an attacker. It can be used to track your online activity, install malware on your computer, or even tell an attacker what operating system you're using – and this applies even while using the encryption offered by TOR or a VPN. The amount of personally identifying information possibly gathered in this way might seem trivial at first glance, but correlations can very quickly snowball until you have a serious problem.

Tails' browser is called Iceweasel, while TOR is usually accessed from Windows by using Firefox. The procedure for changing Javascript settings is exactly the same in either case; open a window and type the following in the address bar: "about:config," clicking the button labeled "I'll be careful, I promise."

You will see a large amount of configuration settings, which you can navigate through with the help of the search bar near the top. Type "Javascript" and you should see two values; "javascript.enabled" and "browser.urlbar.filter.javascript." Click the "toggle" command until both are set to "false." Firefox will remember these settings, but with Tails booting from a USB drive, you will have to check this whenever you start a browsing session.

Blocking Javascript completely is by far the safest, but there are some browser add-ons, which may be suitable for your particular situation. NoScript allows you some control as to which sites are allowed to run scripts, although some people claim that it is not 100% effective. I have no opinion about this. For Firefox or TOR browser, you can look up toggle_js, which lets you enable or disable Javascript by clicking a handy button instead of typing "about:config" each time.

Luckily, Tails and Whonix masks most personally identifying information, assuming you use Tails with JavaScript disabled, or at the very least with NoScripts, giving you the option of drastically reducing the amount of information you share involuntarily. Of course, it is not always possible to use Tails, so Javascript vulnerabilities are something you have to take into account when you are browsing with regular browsers on your native operating system.

See what your browser is revealing about you at this page below. You may wish to search online for other sites that check what information your browser is revealing about you. If you are confident in your computer skills, use the one recommended.

http://browserspy.dk/

Tracking Cookies pose a different kind of threat. It is amazing how much information your browser can reveal about you, without asking your permission or even informing them. Online, cookies are such a common sight that many people no longer care about the risks they can represent. Second-party cookies, if accepted, will be sent to the issuing website every time your browser requests any resource from that webpage. If you remain logged into a website, or you are using functionality that requires several steps (online shopping, filling in multi-page forms), there are cookies involved.

There are also third-party cookies, which only require an advertisement to run on a webpage you visit. Put simply, these tracking cookies are fragments of software added to websites by third parties. This software is then stored on your own computer in order to trace your online behavior, with the possibility of monitoring your behavior on one website or correlating your visits and activity over several different sites. Not only can advertisers, such as Google Ads, then predict what you are likely to buy and choose the ads you see accordingly, but the NSA can also use cookies to compromise your identity:

http://www.washingtonpost.com/blogs/the-switch/wp/2013/12/10/nsa-uses-google-cookies-to-pinpoint-targets-for-hacking/

You might have noticed a similar effect if you've recently searched for, let's say, golf clubs, on Yahoo or Google. Afterward, every website you visit seems to want to sell you a new putter. This is how tracking cookies operate, with their original purpose being targeted marketing based on your interests. That they accomplish this by modifying your computer and spying on you was considered acceptable in some quarters.

Fortunately, TOR, as well as Tails, clears their cookies every time the browser is restarted, though this means you are still being monitored within each browsing session. This function is generally called "session cookies." For example, let's say you post an unflattering comment about a local politician before visiting two or three websites with Google Ads on them (which seems to be most websites, these days). This might sound innocuous, but Google uses this information to construct a model of your browsing behavior: search queries, favorite sites, and so forth. And what if, in a momentary lapse of security mindset, you log into Facebook or webmail while still using the same IP address? Virtually, all of these services are perfectly happy to cooperate with LE, with or without a warrant or even reasonable criminal suspicion. Should you fall into predictable patterns, you might find yourself the subject of an investigation.

Assume that everything you do online will be stored and analyzed, because most of it is. Full information as to how tracking cookies are used to identify individuals is not available, but it is certainly not a good idea to watch a Youtube video of a drone attack, and immediately after visit the webpage of your favorite local restaurant and that of the school your children go to. There are many clever, well-resourced people watching over your shoulder who are capable of figuring these things out; and once you have garnered their suspicion, they have no reason to leave you alone.

Unfortunately, it is not practically possible to disable all cookies. Cookies also serve to identify you to various servers, such as those requiring a login. Without accepting cookies, you will find using such services very difficult. Additionally, new features in web browsers mimic the behavior of cookies without the public being aware of it, nor how to counteract these "stealth cookies."

Adobe Flash has implemented "Local Stored Objects" (or "flash cookies" if you prefer) as a feature of its browser plugin, while Mozilla has added something called "DOM Storage" in the most recent versions of Firefox. Either of these can be used by websites to track visitors without their knowledge.

If you use Firefox, it might be in your interest to turn off DOM storage. Open a browser window, type "about:config" into the address bar, and use the search field to look for "storage." There should be a field called dom.storage.enabled, so set this to "false."

To get rid of Flash cookies, we can start by seeing what Adobe recommends at

http://helpx.adobe.com/flash-player/kb/disable-local-shared-objects-flash.html

One glaring lack is that there is no "session only" configuration option. Instead, it is probably best to set Local Stored Object space to 0 for all websites, and only alter this for pages that you are willing to track you. In the Linux edition of the Flash plugin, I could not find a way to do this for all websites; so be aware of the risk. As mentioned above, Tails does not use Flash, which amongst other things precludes using Youtube. Therefore, if it is truly necessary to watch some video from online, download it using the appropriate browser plugin, store it on your hard drive and watch it from there. That should take care of any Flash cookies.

Monetary transactions, even if they aren't normally regarded as information exchanges, are another hurdle where your security mindset might stumble. Have you ever heard the expression "follow the money"? Think of any of several organized crime figures, who despite leaving piles of dead bodies and ruined lives behind them, are finally brought to trial on tax evasion charges. As a friend of mine put it, you can get away with murder, but don't dare forget about parking tickets!

Until fairly recently, anonymous money exchanges were possible in either small amounts – physical cash – or very large amounts, search for the "Panama Papers" if you don't know what I'm talking about. With the advent of cryptocurrencies, the range in between these extremes is now also available.

We will be talking about Bitcoins, as this is the most popular alternative currency. Firstly, I should explain that Bitcoins are not "as safe as houses." Their rapid growth in both value and popularity has given those in control of fiat currencies mild indigestion, and ordinary (but technically skilled) criminals have also jumped on the bandwagon. Bitcoin exchanges can and have indeed been hacked – you will have to make your own determination about whether it is worse to lose money through an electronic attack, or through force or fraud, and what the relative level of risk is. Unlike, say, the hundred-page mortgage agreement you've signed with your bank, Bitcoins are by design an open system, with the allowed expansion of the money supply carefully defined.

Secondly, I should be clear that I am not advocating breaking the law, if only because this is generally a poor strategy for getting what you want. Any recommendations I make regarding using Bitcoins assumes that you are doing so to safeguard your own security and privacy.

So, let's say you've found something for sale online, and the preferred payment method is Bitcoins. If you've never used them before, you will be asking where you can find some, and how do you send them to your recipient. We'll be examining the various options, and hopefully allow you to make an educated decision on what makes sense for you.

You can search for an online Bitcoin exchange; some well-known enterprises are BTC-E, Bitstamp, and Coinbase. For now, just think of these as banks that deal in Bitcoins rather than Dollars or Euros. Being banks, they will generally require proof of your identity before accepting a wire transfer from a conventional bank to purchase Bitcoins. As such, you've already lost the advantage of anonymity.

Alternatively, LocalBitcoins.com allows you to meet private sellers of Bitcoins based on location. How you conclude the transaction is up to you, whether you send a check, pay by PayPal or meet them in person. Much like a rating on eBay, Bitcoin traders have reputation lists you can view to discourage cheating. Once you've transferred the money by whatever means, the Bitcoins are released (by LocalBitcoins) and will be available in your "wallet." Some users have admitted to apprehension regarding undercover LE operatives posing as traders or buyers, but the fact remains that Bitcoins are not illegal (you will, of course, attract some suspicion if you are trading enormous amounts). If you are truly concerned, a false mustache and a hat may make you feel more at ease.

There are also Bitcoin ATMs in the process of being rolled out, though you will most likely not see one in your area for a while.

http://techcrunch.com/2014/01/02/robocoin-the-bitcoin-atm-is-heading-to-hong-kong-and-taiwan/

"The first shipping bitcoin ATM, Robocoin, is landing in Hong Kong and Taiwan as the company expands its reach this January. They are planning further releases in **Europe, Canada, and the US** *but, given Asia's clout in the BTC markets, this is definitely an interesting development."*

As Bitcoins become more generally accepted as currency for ordinary transactions, and not just online, these ATMs will likely become a valuable convenience for buying and selling small amounts of Bitcoins.

Additionally, you can check the classifieds online or in your local newspaper to see if someone is offering Bitcoins for cash. In this case, you should, of course, take all reasonable precautions against scammers, and against your privacy being violated. Finally, it is possible to "mine" your own Bitcoins – but this is probably more suited to someone with a background in mathematics or computer science.

If you have by now gotten your hands on some Bitcoins, you will probably have read enough to know that every single transaction is logged on BlockChain.info. This is good security, but clearly lousy anonymity. If the whole world can see where your money's been, up to N transactions ago, how do you protect your privacy?

The answer is called a mixer or tumbler. You can imagine it as a giant pile of Bitcoins where every person participating throws a handful of Bitcoins into the center, and then takes back the same amount from another part of the pile. With thousands of people participating, the ownership of any given Bitcoin quickly becomes very difficult to trace beyond the mixer, while their blockchains remain intact. If you are interested in such a service, look up BitcoinFog on either the surface internet or as a hidden service:

http://www.bitcoinfog.com/
http://fogcore5n3ov3tui.onion/

It's best not to forget that this is a commercial entity; your best protection is that they won't want to damage their own reputation. I include them as an example of a mixer service because they have a track record of happy customers. They charge a 1% to 3% commission (the actual figure is selected randomly to make tracing clean Bitcoins even more difficult). It also functions as a bank, allowing you to store your Bitcoins with them for as long as you want. Practically speaking, an interested party will know how many Bitcoins you deposit with them, but tracking the Bitcoins you withdraw will be extremely difficult. Just make sure you send them to a new wallet or ask BitcoinFog to send them directly to your beneficiary.

Blockchain.info itself provides two randomization services, **Send Shared** and **Shared Coin**. The details are different, but the results are similar. As before, the principle, in either case, is to have large numbers of payers and payees involved simultaneously. Your Bitcoins won't be stolen or disappear, and the large number of simultaneous inputs and outputs effectively guarantee anonymity for both sender and receiver. For more detail, visit:

https://blockchain.info

Just hit the button marked "Wallet" to access your existing wallet or sign up. This is all possible using just your browser. But since this book is all about giving you options, I want to introduce you to the Electrum Bitcoin client. Amongst other things, it will protect you from losing coins from a computer blowing up by using a passphrase. It starts pretty quickly because, unlike the standard Bitcoin client (https://bitcoin.org), it does not download the entire blockchain. This is several gigabytes and will only grow larger in future, so budget at least a day's time if you do need to store this locally. We are going to run Electrum on Tails, so start by downloading:

https://download.electrum.org/Electrum-1.9.7.tar.gz

I'm assuming you know how to extract a compressed file, so let's do that. Next, navigate to the extracted directory and type in the following:

```
./electrum -s 56ckl5obj37gypcu.onion:50001:t
-p socks5:localhost:9050
```

You've just asked Electrum to set up a connection over TOR, rather than clearnet. You will see a warning about the connection being potentially unsafe, but you can ignore this; the connection is actually secure. See the following if interested:

https://tails.boum.org/forum/Report:_the_electrum _bitcoin_client_in_tails/

Now we are going to set up your wallet in the directory /tmp/electrum.dat by appending that information to the command above:

```
./electrum -s 56ckl5obj37gypcu.onion:50001:t -
p socks5:localhost:9050 -w /tmp/electrum.dat
```

TOR AND THE DARK NET

Of course, you can also call the file mywallet.dat or whatever you prefer. Whenever you start Electrum with this command, it will know how to connect to TOR and where to look for your wallet. Very importantly, back up your newly created wallet onto removable media for backup. Otherwise, you might lose your entire balance!

This seems to be the easiest way of using Bitcoin from Tails, with the security TOR encryption and anonymity made possible. For further information, visit:

https://electrum.org

I NEED YOUR HELP

I really want to thank you again for reading this book. Hopefully you have liked it so far and have been receiving value from it. Lots of effort was put into making sure that it provides as much content as possible to you and that I cover as much as I can.

If you've found this book helpful, then I'd like to ask you a favor. Would you be kind enough to leave a review for it on Amazon? It would be greatly appreciated!

PART FOUR: WHY THIS IS ALL SO IMPORTANT

How far will Law Enforcement go?

This last part of the book generally deals with less technical topics. Perhaps it should have gone at the beginning of the book rather than the end, or have been left out altogether as being too controversial. Well, if you've picked up this book, you probably understand that your privacy is important even if you're not clear on why; and without a doubt, the ability to discuss controversial topics frankly is one of the reasons why privacy *is* important.

We've already covered a number of fairly complex topics, so now I want to ask you to stretch your mind once more. What I want you to do is simple but perhaps difficult as well: just imagine for a moment that the police force, national security agencies, and the legal system are not like seen on TV. Nor are they like you were taught in school.

I have no doubt that there are many professionals in this field who truly desire safe neighborhoods, an end to terrorism and drug smuggling, and fair trials. I suspect many of these same professionals would agree with me that all is not currently well. A significant portion of "civilians" – as if police are not civilians – feel more threatened than protected by law enforcement, or LE as I've been calling it to name it as a separate concept.

Regrettably, I've come to the conclusion that mere innocence will not protect you from LE. One particularly deplorable example is known as asset forfeiture, whereby the police can confiscate cash, possessions, and even real estate if these are suspected of being the proceeds of crime. The trouble is, as has been demonstrated in numerous cases, that the evidentiary benchmark is a cop saying, "Because I can." Anybody carrying a few thousand in cash is automatically assumed to be a drug dealer, without any other evidence whatsoever. The police need not charge anybody with a crime, and the person who has been robbed – possibly accompanied by various threats – has to somehow prove his innocence instead of the state his guilt.

Furthermore, you need only watch the news to see evidence of abuses of power, incompetence and pernicious amorality at all levels. Large corporations use their financial muscle to overwhelm smaller enterprises; government employees and journalists who expose scandals are persecuted without mercy; a small galaxy of acronymous security agencies routinely violate the law without consequences or even success in their assigned task.

I do not have any specific suggestions on how to fix the world in five easy steps, but I am quite sure that, without practical freedom of conscience and speech, things won't turn out right on their own.

This is why we need PGP and TOR. If you need further encouragement, just look at the following examples to see an illustration of the lengths LE will go to, whether justified or not.

In an ideal world, everybody would obey the law, and we'd expect the same standard from the police. For instance, they are not supposed to plant evidence or enable the commission of a crime.

http://www.usatoday.com/story/news/nation/2013/ 11/07/vendor-administrator-plead-guilty-in-silk-road-case/3469751/

"In April 2012, a DEA undercover agent in Maryland posing as a drug smuggler began communicating with "Dread Pirate Roberts" on Silk Road about selling a large amount of illegal drugs. "Dread Pirate Roberts" instructed [Curtis] Green to help the smuggler find a drug dealer who could buy a large amount of drugs, court papers say.

Green found a buyer and agreed to act as the middleman for a $27,000 sale of a kilogram of cocaine. Green gave the DEA agent his address.

An undercover U.S. Postal Service inspector delivered the cocaine to Green's house in Utah on Jan. 17."

Regardless of your views on trading in illegal drugs, there's something wrong if the police deliver a large quantity of a lethal substance to a drug dealer's front door. It is as if they were willing to do anything, even if it were illegal and could jeopardize their prosecution, to provide evidence against a man they wanted in jail.

Nor is this a unique case: The Secret Service posed as a vendor for fake IDs online for 5 years and actually shipped fake IDs that they made to buyers on an online Russian forum.

http://www.tested.com/tech/456882-how-secret-service-sold-fake-ids-catch-identity-crooks/

"The US Government's "Operation Open Market" resulted in indictments against 55 defendants. According to Wired, Special Agent Mike Adams shipped out more than 125 fake IDs over about five years of activity while going by the username Celtic. Amazingly, the entire scheme started when the government arrested the real Celtic, a Nevada man who got caught shopping at a Whole Foods where he'd previously used a fake credit card.

Law enforcement discovered counterfeiting equipment among his possessions and learned about his online activities. Adams assumed his online identity and even improved Celtic's cred, shipping near-flawless IDs and becoming a trusted seller on Carder.ru."

As you can see in this article, the Secret Service again sold illegal items to people online in order to bust them. Several of the buyers used their real addresses and sent real photos of themselves to this officer to have their IDs made, resulting in being arrested by the feds. We do not know what the false identity documents might have been used for, once they were in the hands of the criminals.

And in this particular case, the feds charged all the defendants under something called the RICO act.

"The main indictment is noteworthy because, in addition to the usual mix of credit card fraud and false identification charges, the 39 defendants have been charged under the mob-busting RICO act – a first for a cybercrime prosecution.

Enacted in 1970 to help the FBI crack down on the mafia, the Racketeer Influenced and Corrupt Organizations Act **lets the feds hold every member of a criminal organization individually responsible for the actions of the group as a whole**. *The losses collectively inflicted by the Carder.ru members are easily enough to give every RICO defendant 20 years in prison."*

So, the lesson is, if you are found guilty of crimes online, especially in an online community, the feds may be able to hold you responsible for the actions of any other user. So, ensure that when you engage in activism, or whatever may you choose to do, you take this into account. Be prepared to be potentially prosecuted under laws meant to be used against large, well-funded, violent organizations, even though none of this describes you. It doesn't look like your actual, individual guilt matters to LE.

https://en.wikipedia.org/wiki/ATF_gunwalking_scandal

The final example we'll look at for now was graced with the gung-ho name "Operation Fast and Furious." The idea was for the ATF to sell firearms to Mexican drug cartels, monitor where the guns went and use this information to arrest crime bosses. Unfortunately, nobody seemed to have thought through the "monitoring" aspect, resulting in about 1,400 weapons going missing on both sides of the border.

As such, what was an obviously bad idea was wholeheartedly embraced by LE professionals, resulting in illegal guns being used in hundreds of crimes. The only rational conclusion is that LE's top priorities may not involve reducing crime.

I believe the theme here is clear. LE is rewarded for arrests and confiscations, not for preventing a crime. They are willing to use less than aboveboard tactics to get their arrests, and it's better for them if you are convicted of a serious crime. Curtis Green is facing up to 40 years in prison, while the people who purchased fake IDs could receive up to 20 years each.

You can raise suspicion in a number of ways, and after that, it can take only a single mistake to be criminally charged. The government has all the guns, most of the computers, and no imperative to play fair. Be careful.

Learning from Others' Mistakes

This chapter will focus on some mistakes that certain "hacktivists" made, leading to their arrests. The group known as LulzSec fitted the mold of pranksters rather than cyber-terrorists or political activists, penetrating corporate servers and leaving sarcastic messages. Their leader referred to himself as Sabu.

https://www.informationweek.com/attacks/lulzsec-leader-sabu-unmasked-aids-fbi-hacker-sweep/d/d-id/1103214?

"The men have been charged with hacking Fox Broadcasting Company, Sony Pictures Entertainment, and the Public Broadcasting Service (aka PBS)."

The group also leaked identity data of Sony users and law enforcement personnel and conducted DDoS (distributed denial of service) attacks on the CIA. In addition, Sabu was accused of selling stolen credit cards online. The FBI wanted him on charges that could have gotten him 112 years' imprisonment – which seems rather harsh for nonviolent crimes and is significantly more than sentences handed down for many major financial frauds.

http://www.foxnews.com/tech/2012/03/06/exclusive-unmasking-worlds-most-wanted-hacker/

*"Sabu had always been cautious, hiding his Internet protocol address through proxy servers. But then just once he slipped. He logged into an Internet relay chatroom from his own IP address without masking it. **All it took was once.** The feds had a fix on*

him."

In fact, though this was the incident that identified him to the FBI, Sabu had made a major mistake previously. This was noticed by a rival hacking group called Backtrace, who posted his identity weeks before:

http://arstechnica.com/tech-policy/2012/03/doxed-how-sabu-was-outed-by-former-anons-long-before-his-arrest/

"Sabu occasionally mentioned ownership of a domain called prvt.org in his chats, including those in Backtrace's "consequences" document. Every domain registration is associated with corresponding information in the WHOIS database. This information is supposed to include the name and address of the domain's owner.

Often this information is incorrect (most domain registrars do nothing to validate it) or anonymized (many firms offer "proxy" domain registration, so the WHOIS database contains the details of the proxy registrar, rather than the person using the domain). Monsegur appeared to use one of these anonymizing services, Go Daddy Subsidiary Domains by Proxy, for registering the prvt.org domain.

The registration for the domain was due to expire on June 25, 2011, requiring Monsegur (Sabu) to renew it. But for some reason—error on Monsegur's part perhaps, or screw-up by the registrar—the renewal was processed not by Domains by Proxy but by its parent, Go Daddy. Unlike Domains by Proxy, Go Daddy uses real information when it updates the WHOIS database, so on 24th June (the day before it was due to expire), **Monsegur's name, address, and telephone number were all publicly attached to his domain name.**

Monsegur quickly remedied the mistake, changing the WHOIS registration to use various other identities—first to that of Adrian Lamo (who reported Bradley Manning to authorities) and then to

"Rafael Lima" and subsequently to "Christian Biermann." This attempt to mislead those relying on the WHOIS information successfully misled some would-be doxers. But not all: by August there were extensive dossiers on Sabu's true identity."

So, these two mistakes – or either one of them – were all that was required to end the career of the most wanted hacker in the world at that time. But the story does not end for Sabu yet:

*"An unemployed computer programmer, welfare recipient and **legal guardian of two young children.***

"It was because of his kids," one of the two agents recalled. "He'd do anything for his kids. He didn't want to go away to prison and leave them. That's how we got him."

*Monsegur was quietly arrested on aggravated identity theft charges and released on bail. On Aug. 15 he pleaded guilty to a dozen counts of hacking-related charges and **agreed to cooperate with the FBI."***

"Agreed to cooperate," of course, meant that he would help the feds to arrest his former colleagues.

http://arstechnica.com/tech-policy/2012/03/stakeout-how-the-fbi-tracked-and-busted-a-chicago-anon/

*"The day after Christmas, sup_g had another online chat about the Stratfor hack and about some 30,000 credit card numbers that had been taken from the company. His interlocutor, **CW-1**, engaged in a bit of gallows humor about what might happen should they all get caught.*

*But the raid had, in fact, already happened. **CW-1 was "Sabu,"** a top Anon/LulzSec hacker who was in real life an unemployed 28-year old living in New York City public housing. His sixth-floor apartment had been visited by the FBI in June 2011, and Sabu had been arrested and "turned." For months, he had been an FBI informant, watched 24 hours a day by an agent and using a government issued laptop that logged everything he did."*

So, we see here Sabu is chatting with a user **sup_g** to try to have him speak about recent exploits.

*"Sabu suddenly addresses sup_g by a new name, "anarchaos." It would turn out that sup_g went by many names, including "anarchaos," "**burn**," "yohoho," "POW," "tylerknowsthis," and "crediblethreat."*

*CW-1: if I get raided, **anarchaos** your job is to cause havoc in my honor*

CW-1:   *<3*
CW-1:   *sup_g:*
@sup_g: it shall be so

Normally, the attempt to link his various names would have raised the hacker's guard; as he confided to Sabu, someone else had once tried to link the names "*yohoho*" and "**burn**," but the hacker "never answered... I think he picked up some language similarities I've worked with [REDACTED] on other ops in the past." But this was Sabu, a sort of hacker demigod in the world of Anonymous. If you couldn't trust him, who could you trust? Sabu had even provided a server to store the stolen Stratfordata so he couldn't be a fed (in reality, **he had done so at the FBI's direction**)."

With a large amount of previously stored data, there was more than enough to tie user **sup_g** to his real identity.

"*To identify sup_g, the Bureau first turned to the voluminous chat logs stored on Sabu's computer. They went through every comment that could be plausibly linked to sup_g or one of his aliases. The goal was to see if the hacker had slipped up at any point and revealed some personal information.*

He had. On August 29, 2011, at 8:37 AM, "**burn**" said in an IRC channel that "some comrades of mine were arrested in St. Louis a few weeks ago... for midwestrising tar sands work." If accurate, this might place "**burn**" in the Midwest. FBI Chicago agents were able to confirm that an event called Midwest Rising was attended by Chicago resident Jeremy Hammond's twin brother. (Hammond had a history of anarchism and violent protest).

"Anarchaos" once let slip that he had been arrested in 2004 for protesting at the Republican National Convention in New York City. Much later, "yohoho" noted that he hadn't been to New York "since the RNC," nicely tying both online handles to the same person. The FBI went to New York City police and obtained a list of every individual detained at the 2004 convention; they learned that Jeremy Hammond had, in fact, been detained, though he had not been arrested. The pieces were starting to fit.

"Sup_g" and "**burn**" both indicated later that they had spent time in prison, with "**burn**" indicating that he had been in a federal penitentiary. A search of Hammond's criminal records revealed that he had been arrested in March 2005 by the Chicago FBI and had pled guilty to hacking into a "politically conservative website and stealing its computer database, including credit card information," according to an FBI affidavit. Hammond was sentenced to two years in prison for the action.

In yet another chat, "**Anarchaos**" told Sabu that he had once spent a few weeks in a county jail for possession of marijuana. He also asked Sabu not to tell *anybody, "cause it could compromise my identity," and he noted that he was on probation. Both matched Hammond, who was placed on probation in November 2010 after a violent protest against the Olympics coming to Chicago. When the FBI ran a criminal history check on Hammond, it also revealed two arrests for marijuana possession.*

The FBI was so thorough that it even followed up on a "POW" comment saying "dumpster diving is all good I'm a freegan goddess." ("Freegans" scavenge unspoiled, wasted food from the trash of grocery stores and restaurants). The FBI went to Chicago authorities, who had put Hammond under surveillance when they were investigating him back in 2005. As part of that earlier surveillance, "agents have seen Hammond going into dumpsters to get food."

Now that they had a suspect, it was time to put him under surveillance."

This illustrates the dangers of giving out even apparently inconsequential personal information over the internet. A few legal embarrassments, perhaps a reference to a town you used to live in, and an unusual diet can be enough for you to be 90% positively identified. It would have been worth his while to assume that LE could put assemble these breadcrumbs into a trail.

"Watching the WiFi network revealed the Media Access Control (MAC) addresses of each device connected to the network. Most of the time there was only one, an Apple Computer—and sup_g had told Sabu that he used a MacBook.

On March 1, the agents obtained a court order allowing them to use a "pen register/trap and trace" device that could reveal only "addressing information" and not content. In other words, if it worked, agents could see what IP addresses Hammond was visiting, but they would see nothing else.

His MacBook's MAC address was soon seen connecting to IP addresses known to be part of the Tor anonymizing network.

And while this definitely sounded like their man, the Bureau went to even greater lengths to double-check their target. The main technique was to observe when Hammond left his home, then to call Sabu in New York and ask if any of Hammond's suspected aliases had just left IRC or the Jabber instant messaging system."

Remember that everything you say online is probably stored, maybe indefinitely. This applies equally to things you didn't consciously say, such as the times you've logged into a server with your real IP address. Should you one day attract suspicion for something you can't even imagine today, all of this comes together; and the fact that it's only circumstantial evidence might not help you at all.

Security, Servers, and Subpoenas

You should not underestimate the resources available to LE when it comes to anyone they regard as a person of interest. You only need to screw up once, and they will make sure you have no secrets from them.

Quite a large number of corporations you might entrust your data to, would be just as happy to turn your information over to "proper authority" without much more than an informal request, so be especially careful with any information posted to a service supported by advertising. In particular, there's no reason to discuss the Deep Web on social media; this will only interest LE in what you might be using TOR for.

Even if an online service you use respects your privacy (for example, by not logging IP addresses), a court order might force them to start monitoring your activity. Hush Mail was forced to hand over 12 CDs worth of emails from three email accounts:

http://www.wired.com/threatlevel/2007/11/encrypted-e-mai/

When threatened with bankruptcy or even imprisonment, 99% of companies will do what they're told. There was a notable exception to this rule recently, called LavaBit:

http://www.theguardian.com/world/2013/oct/03/lavabit-ladar-levison-fbi-encryption-keys-snowden

*"The email service used by whistleblower **Edward Snowden** refused FBI requests to "defeat its own system," according to newly unsealed court documents.*

*The founder of LavaBit, **Ladar Levison**, repeatedly pushed back against demands by the authorities to hand over the encryption keys to his system, frustrating federal investigators who were trying to track Snowden's communications, the documents show.*

***Levison** is now subject to a government gag order and has appealed against the search warrants and subpoenas demanding access to his service. He closed LavaBit in August saying he did not want to be "complicit in crimes against the*

American people."

In July, the authorities obtained a search warrant demanding LavaBit hand over any encryption keys and SSL keys that protected the site. Levison was threatened with criminal contempt – which could have potentially put him in jail – if he did not comply. Such a move would have given the government access to all of LavaBit users' information.

The court ordered Levison to be fined $5,000 a day beginning 6 August until he handed over electronic copies of the keys. Two days later Levison handed over the keys, hours after he shuttered LavaBit."

This is Orwellian that a businessman is ordered by the government to compromise the privacy of half a million users, so they could gain more information on one man. Not only that but used strong-arm tactics and punitive fines and finally forced him to close his business. Even worse than that, he was not allowed to explain why he had no choice but to shut down LavaBit.

If all that was not sufficiently insane, Levison later revealed that similar businesses were forced to keep operating so that LE could continue to monitor their users.

http://www.theregister.co.uk/2013/11/19/lavabit_a nalysis/

"Lavabit's founder has claimed other secure webmail providers who threatened to shut themselves down in the wake of the NSA spying revelations had received court orders forcing them to stay up."

Imagine yourself in this scenario for a moment. You are a completely innocent businessman. You have the relevant licenses, you pay your taxes, and you stop at traffic lights. One day, without being charged or suspected of a crime, without being accused of being an accomplice to a crime – which would be difficult, since no actual crime had been committed, and if it had been, you wouldn't have known about it, much less offered assistance – without even a hint of wrongdoing on your part, the government one day decides to seize your livelihood, ruin your reputation, and potentially put you in jail. You would not be happy about it, I think.

Like a Kafka story, when you think it can't, it only gets worse. You are not allowed to appeal; you are not even allowed to speak about what is being done to you. If you are so morally offended by what they are forcing you to do that you prefer killing your own business to cooperating with an abusive system, they can tell you: "No, you work for us now without pay and without ever choosing to do so, and you're not allowed to stop until we don't need you to spy on people who trust you on our behalf, anymore. At that point, don't even think about opening your mouth, or coming to us for help."

You might have smirked at the idea of burly men in cheap suits coming to your house one day, breaking down the door, and confiscating all your electronic hardware. Does it still seem like an unreasonable fear? Remember, the government – which really is shorthand for "anybody who works for the government" – can do whatever they want. If they don't want to do bad things to you, it just means you aren't yet worth their trouble.

You should also not assume that LE will bother with the formality of a search warrant if this does not suit them. The US government is the largest purchaser of malware in the world.

http://endthelie.com/2013/05/10/report-us-government-now-buys-more-malware-than-anyone-else-in-the-world/#axzz2qIjeZ32e

"According to a new report, the United States government is now, in fact, the single largest buyer of malware in the world thanks to the shift to "offensive" cybersecurity and is leaving us all vulnerable in the process.

In order for the government to exploit vulnerabilities discovered in major software, they cannot disclose those vulnerabilities to the manufacturers or the public, lest the exploit be fixed.

"My job was to have 25 zero-days on a USB stick, ready to go," one former executive at a defense contractor told Reuters. The defense contractor would purchase vulnerabilities from independent hackers and then turn them into exploits for the government to use as an offensive cyberweapon."

Unlike our earlier examples of LE selling false IDs and guns to criminals, in this case, the government is essentially paying criminals for illegal software. Independent hackers can earn more than $ 100,000 for finding a zero-day exploit – vulnerabilities, which aren't publicly known.

All computers are somehow vulnerable to software attack. John MacAfee, the founder of MacAfee anti-virus, explains:

""We don't have much [security] anymore, and certainly not in the online world," he said at Saturday's talk. "If you can give me just any small amount of information about yourself, I promise you, within three days, I can turn on the camera on your computer at home and watch whatever you're doing.""

http://abcnews.go.com/Technology/john-mcafees-product-aims-make-internet-users-virtually/story?id=20424182

So, one reasonable thing to do is to put some electrician's tape over your webcam and disconnect any microphones, but this will only stop a hacker from seeing what you are currently doing. Your data remains vulnerable to hackers of both the official and independent varieties.

Below is a description of a keystroke logging malware program developed by the FBI, called Magic Lantern. It can be installed without physical access to your computer:

https://en.wikipedia.org/wiki/Magic_Lantern_%28 software%29

"The FBI intends to deploy Magic Lantern in the form of an e-mail attachment. When the attachment is opened, it installs a trojan horse on the suspect's computer. **The trojan horse is activated when the suspect uses PGP encryption, often used to increase the security of sent e-mail messages. When activated, the trojan horse will log the PGP password, which allows the FBI to decrypt user communications.** Spokesmen for the FBI soon confirmed the existence of a program called Magic Lantern. They denied that it had been deployed, and they declined to comment further."

If that does not scare you sufficiently:

"Mobile phone (cell phone) microphones can be activated remotely, without any need for physical access. This "roving bug" feature has been used by law enforcement agencies and intelligence services to listen in on nearby conversations."

https://en.wikipedia.org/wiki/Covert_listening_devi ce#Remotely_activated_mobile_phone_microphone s

This can be used to listen to your phone conversations, but works equally well when the phone is not connected, or off. If somebody might have managed to infiltrate your phone in this way, the best thing to do is to keep it around while you are not discussing anything sensitive and leave it with the battery removed in another room for any talk you're not comfortable sharing with the world. Also, remember that your phone's position can be instantly and accurately triangulated from either real or simulated base stations. The first group of people, who went to meet with Snowden in Russia were not allowed to bring cell phones or laptops with them, for exactly these reasons.

Put this way, the situation seems pretty grim, with ordinary citizens on one side and a massively resourced LE organization with zero scruples on the other. So, how can we possibly protect ourselves?

The first thing is not to panic. Even with their frightening ability to intercept and store virtually all electronic communication, their analysis capacity remains limited. If you are not currently on their radar and take reasonable precautions, you're likely to keep it that way. Secure your computers as best you can by taking precautions, such as disabling Javascript. In the medium turn, start learning to use Linux in preference to Windows or Mac. The Linux source code is reviewed by many talented programmers, and therefore, any security flaw is much more likely to be spotted and fixed than in a proprietary operating system.

Not browsing the internet without using a virtual machine, such as a virtual box, provides you with a definite security advantage. If you absolutely have to visit dubious websites, consider keeping a secondary computer without any important data on it. Do not open email attachments you weren't definitely expecting, and keep any defense software patched and updated, and the same with the BIOS, which is the software that runs even before your operating system.

If you've managed to really attract LE's attention, there is little you can do to maintain your privacy after that point; most of the advice in this book is intended to avoid exactly that situation. They might use, for instance, *Tempest* attacks that monitor electromagnetic emissions from your equipment. Watch the following video for clarification, and as an exercise, remember that your watching it will probably be recorded.

http://www.dailymotion.com/embed/video/x74iq0

So, anyone who can afford the technology can park outside your house and analyze what you are typing, even over a wired keyboard. With just a little bit more sophistication, they can intercept the video signals to your screen as well, and see what you are seeing. According to the people involved in the experiment, they were able to read wired keyboard signals from up to 20 meters away without specialized equipment. They go on to explain that wireless keyboards and mice are even more susceptible since they transmit intentionally.

"Microsoft has upgraded the weak encryption found on today's mass-market wireless keyboards with a new design that uses 128-bit AES to secure communication to and from the PC.

Hitherto, keyboard encryption has been weak, with keys chosen from a small palette of possibilities, **with one hacking group claiming in 2009 that it had developed a tool specifically to sniff keystrokes from Microsoft keyboards at a range up to 10 meters."**

http://news.techworld.com/security/3284218/new-microsoft-wireless-keyboard-gets-128-bit-encryption/

For reference, 10 meters is approximately 30 feet, but high-level, sophisticated equipment could increase the receiving distance significantly. In another experiment, one researcher was able to intercept a "smart" electricity meter's signal from 900 feet away. She could then figure out which house it was installed in and if anybody was home, based on power consumption.

"The data sent was in plain text and carried the identification number of the meter and its reading. The name of the homeowner or the address aren't included, but anyone motivated enough could quickly figure out the source.

"The meter ID was printed on the front of the meter we looked at, so theoretically you could read the ID [off a target meter] and try to sniff packets," Xu said.

In her tests, Xu found she was able to pull packets out of the air from target meters between once every 2 to 10 minutes. That's fast enough to be able to work out the average power consumption of a house and notice start to deduce when someone is at home."

https://www.networkworld.com/news/2012/11051 2-smart-meters-not-so-clever-263977.html

There are few things you can do to defeat an attack of this kind, though the following website has some suggestions:

http://www.lessemf.com/smart.html

"Y-SHIELD

YShield High-Frequency Shielding Paint

Easy to apply water-based paint for walls, ceilings, doors and other interior OR exterior surfaces. Very effective for blocking cell phone signals, CB, TV, AM, FM signals, radiofrequency radiation, and microwaves. Tested highly effective up to 18 GHz!"

I may be wrong, but based on the quotation above, I don't think they know quite how radio waves work.

Aside from spooks crouched in vans in front of your house, there is another kind of sophisticated attack that requires physical access to your computer. We'll assume that you've implemented whole disk encryption, haven't written down your password where somebody can find it, and adhered to all the good practices we've described.

There is still a potential vulnerability in the form of your RAM. Without going into detail, your computer's RAM is its short-term, fast access memory. It really is much, much faster to use than (say) a hard disk, but doesn't retain its data without power.

That is, RAM generally doesn't remember what is stored on it for longer than a few milliseconds without power, but this can vary. If your computer is powered up and you are working on some file, that file is stored in RAM without any encryption applied to it. If the RAM is now cooled to somewhere below zero before being disconnected, it may remember the unencrypted data for up to several minutes. This is known as a "cold boot attack." Modern DRAM does not even have to be cooled for this to be possible, the name is from earlier generations of components.

At least one group of researchers was able to recover cryptographic keys using this method. In their own words:

"Lest We Remember: Cold Boot Attacks on Encryption Keys
Abstract.

Contrary to popular assumption, DRAMs used in most modern computers retain their contents for seconds to minutes after power is lost, even at operating temperatures and even if removed from a motherboard. Although DRAMs become less reliable when they are not refreshed, they are not immediately erased, and their contents persist sufficiently for malicious (or forensic) acquisition of usable full-system memory images. We show that this phenomenon limits the ability of an operating system to protect cryptographic key material from an attacker with physical access. We use cold reboots to mount attacks on popular disk encryption systems — BitLocker, FileVault, dm-crypt, and TrueCrypt — using no special devices or materials. We experimentally characterize the extent and predictability of memory remanence and report that remanence times can be increased dramatically with simple techniques. We offer new algorithms for finding cryptographic keys in memory images and for correcting errors caused by bit decay. Though we discuss several strategies for partially mitigating these risks, we know of no simple remedy that would eliminate them."

https://citp.princeton.edu/research/memory/

[Abstract]   http://citpsite.s3-website-us-east-

1.amazonaws.com/oldsite-htdocs/pub/coldboot.pdf
[Full Text]

Practically speaking, assuming that someone barges into your home or workplace, gets access to your computer while still powered up and displaying otherwise-encrypted information on the screen, with the necessary hardware to search the RAM chips for encryption keys all ready to go, you already have so many problems that one more won't make a difference. Nevertheless, this is a good example of a sophisticated hardware attack. Let's see what encryption software TrueCrypt's developers have to say about the implications:

"Unencrypted Data in RAM

It is important to note that TrueCrypt is disk encryption software, which encrypts only disks, not RAM (memory).

Keep in mind that most programs do not clear the memory area (buffers) in which they store unencrypted (portions of) files they load from a TrueCrypt volume. This means that after you exit such a program, unencrypted data it worked with may remain in memory (RAM) until the computer is turned off (and, according to some researchers, even for some time after the power is turned off*). Also note that if you open a file stored on a TrueCrypt volume, for example, in a text editor and then force dismount on the TrueCrypt volume, then the file will remain unencrypted in the area of memory (RAM) used by (allocated to) the text editor. This applies to forced auto-dismount too.

Inherently, unencrypted master keys have to be stored in RAM too. When a non-system TrueCrypt volume is dismounted, TrueCrypt erases its master keys (stored in RAM). When the computer is cleanly restarted (or cleanly shut down), all non-system TrueCrypt volumes are automatically dismounted and, thus, all master keys stored in RAM are erased by the TrueCrypt driver (except master keys for system partitions/drives — see below). However, when power supply is abruptly interrupted, when the computer is reset (not cleanly restarted), or when the system crashes, TrueCrypt naturally stops running and therefore cannot erase any keys or any other sensitive data. Furthermore, as Microsoft does not provide any appropriate API for handling hibernation and shutdown, master keys used for system encryption cannot be reliably (and are not) erased from RAM when the computer hibernates, is shut down or restarted.**."

To summarize, TrueCrypt cannot and does not ensure that RAM contains no sensitive data (e.g. passwords, master keys, or decrypted data). Therefore, after each session in which you work with a TrueCrypt volume or in which an encrypted operating system is running, you must shut down (or, if the hibernation file is encrypted, hibernate) the computer and then leave it powered off for at least several minutes (the longer, the better) before turning it on again. This is required to clear the RAM.

* Allegedly, for 1.5-35 seconds under normal operating temperatures (26-44 °C) and up to several hours when the memory modules are cooled (when the computer is running) to very low temperatures (e.g. -50 °C). New types of memory modules allegedly exhibit a much shorter decay time (e.g. 1.5-2.5 seconds) than older types (as of 2008).

** Before a key can be erased from RAM, the corresponding TrueCrypt volume must be dismounted. For non-system volumes, this does not cause any problems. However, as Microsoft currently does not provide any appropriate API for handling the final phase of the system shutdown process, paging files located on encrypted system volumes that are dismounted during the system shutdown process may still contain valid swapped-out memory pages (including portions of Windows system files). This could cause 'blue screen' errors. Therefore, to prevent 'blue screen' errors, TrueCrypt does not dismount encrypted system volumes and consequently cannot clear the master keys of the system volumes when the system is shut down or restarted."

http://www.truecrypt.org/docs/unencrypted-data-in-ram

(Note: TrueCrypt is no longer recommended as an encryption tool due to unnamed issues).

One scenario where this attack might present a realistic problem is where you use whole-disk encryption for your system partition. The reason for this is that the master key to this partition remains in RAM from the moment you log on until the moment you shut down, and can potentially be used to access the entire disk. If you decide to follow this route, consider keeping truly sensitive data on a separate partition or removable drive, which you can mount and unmount as needed.

PART FIVE: FINAL WORDS

So, you've done your homework, read up to here, and secured your computer use as best you can. Yet, that still may not be enough. It might involve nothing more sinister than being seen at the wrong place at the wrong time, or having an acquaintance you didn't know was up to no good. In case this ever happens to you, the following information might just save you a ton of grief.

The Strength of Cryptography and Anonymity when Used Properly

Before we start talking about worst-case scenarios, let's review an example of pure "black-hat" (evil, done for personal gain) hacking. It is called ransomware, and one particular virus called CryptoLocker.

What it does is lock you out of your own computer, denying you access to your half-finished thesis, the quarterly report due next week, or even your Minesweeper high scores. According to Dell SecureWorks, upwards of a quarter-million users have been infected. The average amount extorted is $ 300 (that's $ 75 million total), and millions in laundered Bitcoins have been traced to the gang's "mules" who move the money. (On a related note, if you get spam promising you a weekly payment for doing nothing, you are possibly being solicited for this role).

Having turned up from late 2013, CryptoLocker may spread as an email attachment, amongst other things, and attacks Microsoft Windows. In this case, a compressed file contains an executable file with the filename and icon disguised as a PDF. Assuming that you are only half-awake at the time and security is the farthest thing from your mind, you might end up executing the attachment without thinking.

As soon as you do this, the trojan is activated and starts encrypting selected files on both local and mapped network drives. This is done using 2048-bit RSA public-private key encryption, and the catch is, the private key is only stored on servers controlled by the malware's authors.

The victim is then prompted to pay the ransom by a stated deadline, using either Bitcoin or a similarly untraceable instrument. If you do not meet the deadline, the private key will be deleted, and you will have a snowball's chance of ever recovering your data. In fact, if the deadline passes you get another chance to cough up your hard-earned money, but for a substantially increased ransom.

I don't need to point out that this is a reprehensible scheme, targeting the poor and rich without distinction. From a purely technical perspective, however, it is highly successful. To date, nobody infected has managed to defeat BitLocker. The police department of Swansea, Massachusetts was attacked in November and found that they had no option but to pay 2 Bitcoin, about $ 750 in tax money, or potentially lose months of work.

What this is supposed to illustrate is not the potential in becoming a cybercriminal, but the power of strong encryption and careful anonymity. CryptoLocker uses 2,048-bit encryption and has not been beaten yet. If you use the same or longer key lengths, your information should be perfectly safe against any kind of expected attack. Furthermore, the gang used suitable means of online anonymity to safely receive more than BTC 40,000, according to research done by:

http://www.zdnet.com/cryptolockers-crimewave-a-trail-of-millions-in-laundered-bitcoin-7000024579/

"In research for this article ZDnet traced four bitcoin addresses posted (and re-posted) in forums by multiple CryptoLocker victims, showing movement of 41,928 BTC between October 15 and December 18.

Based on the current Bitcoin value of $661, the malware ninjas have moved $27,780,000 through those four addresses alone — if CryptoLocker cashes out today.

If CryptoLocker's supervillains cash out when Bitcoin soars back up to $1000, like it did on November 27… Well, $41.9 million isn't bad for three months of work."

(Note the disparity between the figures of $ 75 million and $ 42 million, that means that almost half the victims paid the ransom. Have backups, people!)

If a gang of international criminals can become rich and remain faceless using some of the techniques described in this book, these techniques have a fair chance of working for you, too.

Retaining a Lawyer, and what to do if Interrogated

We both hope you will not be accused of a crime, but being innocent is no defense against this. Once you are in police custody, or even only on their radar, the chances of a conviction in court, a forced plea-bargain or other sanction go up dramatically.

If LE has decided, for their own reasons, that you are worth bringing in, there is little you can do proactively at that point. For this reason, if you can possibly afford it, do the following:

"Give your lawyer 50k and put him on a retainer.

Don't have an emergency fund 'stash' lying around if that is what you mean…. you should already have your lawyer paid + plus extra in case he needs to post bond for you, and they seize the majority of your drug funds."

This advice refers to somebody who is actually a drug dealer but applies to law-abiding citizens as well. As seen previously in this book, the way asset forfeiture laws are interpreted can mean that just having an emergency fund can be seen as prima facie evidence of goodness-knows-what, and will most likely end up in the police's coffers instead of a defense lawyer's hands. So it might just be worthwhile to have a substantial amount of money sitting in your lawyer's trust account, or at least explore the possibilities of taking out legal insurance.

Next, assume you've been escorted to the "box," and they start asking you questions. Do not think that you are not facing experts and do not think they care more about justice than getting a conviction. Their best outcome is to walk out with a confession, and they will use a variety of tactics on you. While it is unlikely that you'll be physically hurt, they are allowed to lie to you, play on your fears and any guilt you might be feeling, threaten to destroy your reputation or take your children away from you, charge you with a more serious crime than they actually suspect you of, send you to a prison for violent offenders…the confession, or even any indication you know what they're talking about, is all they are after. They might offer to let you go if you can implicate someone else – but they are probably not going to let you go if you admit even to suspecting a friend of something illegal.

So, do not cooperate. If they wanted cooperation, they could have asked before handcuffing and abducting you. In their eyes, of course, you are now being difficult, and they will turn up the intensity of the interrogation. Make no mistake, this will continue for hours at a time, and few people can maintain their cool under such pressure.

So, be prepared for scare tactics and *keep your mouth shut*. They will tell you that giving them whatever they want is to your advantage, that they are really trying to help you; both of these are untrue. Continue to ask for a lawyer even if they say that this will make you look guilty, or that any "generous offers" they've made you will expire once you have legal representation. A lawyer makes their job harder by forcing them to follow the law, so they'll try to prevent this from happening. If you have the right to remain silent, and somebody else is not in immediate danger, exercise that right.

Apart from the above, don't be abusive or surly with the cops; this will convince them that you're guilty faster than any amount of hard evidence. Don't argue with them about the evidence they claim to have, and don't even let them draw you into a conversation. Take comfort in the fact that if they did have solid evidence against you or a friend, they would never need to grill you this hard.

In the absence of solid evidence, they will try to intimidate you with the circumstantial kind. They might try to build up a framework to hang your "bad character" on by correlating financial information from your bank, packages delivered to your home, day trips you took out of town, all forms of communication, a ten-year-old arrest at a political rally; any way they can think of to connect you to whatever they want to put you in jail for. Just remember that the most damning piece of evidence possible is a confession, no matter under what circumstances it was obtained.

So, retain a lawyer, and be honest with him. He or she will not share any information you tell him/her with LE and legally is not allowed to except under extraordinary circumstances. Talk to them, find out what the evidence against you actually is, and have them present during any subsequent interviews with police.

https://en.wikipedia.org/wiki/Attorney%E2%80%93client_privilege#When_the_privilege_may_not_apply

Capabilities of the NSA

Now we've dealt with the sadly relevant issue of being arrested without any real evidence against you, it is time to examine how such evidence may be gathered. This video by Jacob Applebaum, a TOR developer, explains many of these aspects better than I can, and it is highly recommended. None of what is mentioned is a paranoid conspiracy theory or even informed speculation; it is all a confirmed fact. In case you are still not convinced of the need for security mindset, you certainly should make time to see this (it is about an hour long).

You may watch the video on YouTube using HTML5 embeds instead of Flash:

https://youtu.be/vILAlhwUgIU

A Few Recommendations

We've already covered the basics and more, but there are still a few general tips that might not be obvious unless you think about them.

If you have a computer containing sensitive information, do not let others use it. This should really be a part of etiquette in the modern age. I've had people I know ask me urgently to use my PC "just for a few emails"; when I see it again, it's running slower due to malware having infected it, software I don't want nor recognize has been installed, and so forth. Worse, let's say you are connected to a VPN over TOR as a standard security precaution (that is, YOU -> TOR -> VPN -> WWW). This means that the VPN address is where your packet data enters the internet. Now, what happens if your child or spouse uses that connection to log into Facebook? Immediately, you are associated with that VPN, and possibly with any traffic you might have used it for previously.

Your friends and loved ones may just not care about what I've termed security mindset, so if necessary, you might want to keep an outdated computer around just for guests to use. Keep your actual computer password locked at a minimum and consider physically locking it in place.

Unless you are sure that a friend feels the same about issues as you do, it's best not to discuss them. Despite all the technical surveillance going on, we are not quite at the point where friends and family are encouraged or required to inform on each other, but this may happen in future. I'm thinking of the period immediately after the Second World War when LE was investigating possible security breaches in the atomic weapons program. They started out by asking the scientists involved, "Who on your team is a Communist?" which quickly turned into, "Who might be a Communist?" and ended up as, "If anybody might be a Communist, who would it be?" Lives were ruined for no reason, and with no gain in security. If your friend can honestly say "Dunno" to all the above, you are both protected.

use the same password for several online accounts, marketplaces, bulletin boards, and the rest. As we've seen, malicious Javascript can potentially divert your passwords to unintended recipients, and that doesn't If you use several levels of protection to connect, like a VPN over TOR as above, check from time to time that all are still in place. A VPN connection can terminate without you even knowing. In my opinion, this is one advantage of Tortilla: if the TOR segment of the connection ceases to function, Tortilla does not find an alternate route but stops working completely. There are a number of websites you can visit to find out what IP address it "sees" on your traffic.

Finally, do not even count the possibility that one of your regular websites is either careless with your details. The only times I personally use the same, weak password is for websites that require a login but have absolutely no information about me. This login is different from my real name and connects to a webmail account that I can afford to have spammed to death.

One way to choose a strong password is to take a dictionary and choose four words at random; this is actually more resistant to brute-force attacks than including a number, and you should be able to find a way to remember something like "Nimble likable food nostalgic."

Absolute Last Resorts

Let's imagine, for one terrifying moment, that your position has become completely untenable. You have no option but to disappear as completely as you can, and as soon as possible. The following paragraph lists the countries that do not have an extradition treaty with the USA:

Afghanistan, Algeria, Andorra, Angola, Armenia, Bahrain, Bangladesh, Belarus, Bosnia and Herzegovina, Brunei, Burkina Faso, Burma, Burundi, Cambodia, Cameroon, Cape Verde, the Central African Republic, Chad, China, Comoros, Congo (Kinshasa), Congo (Brazzaville), Djibouti, Equatorial Guinea, Eritrea, Ethiopia, *Former Yugoslav Republic* of *Macedonia*, Gabon, Guinea, Guinea-Bissau, Indonesia, Ivory Coast, Kazakhstan, Kosovo, Kuwait, Laos, Lebanon, Libya, Madagascar, Maldives, Mali, Marshall Islands, Mauritania, Micronesia, Moldova, Mongolia, Montenegro, Morocco, Mozambique, Namibia, Nepal, Niger, Oman, Qatar, Russia, Rwanda, Samoa, São Tomé & Príncipe, Saudi Arabia, Senegal, Serbia, Somalia, Sudan, Syria, Togo, Tunisia, Uganda, Ukraine, United Arab Emirates, Uzbekistan, Vanuatu, The Vatican, Vietnam and Yemen.

Now, that does not mean that they will not extradite you under any circumstances, but at least it will not be automatic. Keep in mind, you do not have to be proven guilty for an extradition request to be granted, it only has to be proven that you might be guilty. Edward Snowden and Julian Assange could probably tell you all about it. They've each managed to find an uncertain sanctuary for the moment, but their futures look bleak as long as the US LE (through a Swedish proxy in Assange's case) remains out for blood.

It seems to be a hobby of some US citizens to threaten to "move to Canada" as soon as they no longer feel welcome in their mother country. This is short-sighted; if you are wanted for anything remotely criminal (or as mentioned above, even wanted for questioning), you'll probably be on the next flight. It is legal to sell cannabis seeds within Canada, but one online vendor, a Canadian citizen, who sent this product to customers in the US was extradited to serve a five-year sentence. On the other hand, in at least one case of kidnapping by a parent, the American protectorate Costa Rica actually granted a fleeing woman asylum:

http://www.usatoday.com/news/topstories/2008-07-25-3841863361_x.htm

"Tomayko's claims that her actions were justified by domestic violence she suffered were taken into account by the Costa Rican authorities."

So, in practical terms, a lot will depend on your particular circumstances, whether there's a political angle for the country you wish to flee to, etc. If you are in actual, serious, immediate trouble, this ultimate option to preserve your personal liberty will be difficult to exercise. Look at the list of countries above, for starters: Afghanistan, Saudi Arabia, and Syria do not have the best reputation for human rights. Even before you get there, there is the problem of booking a flight, getting some money together, and transporting it to your new destination (do not take cash), perhaps obtaining a passport, and a hundred other details.

This kind of sums up the theme of this book: avoid getting into trouble by hiding your identity, your online activity, and sometimes even your opinions.

Conclusion

This book has been very interesting to research and write, and I hope that all of you have learned something. Even if you aren'tgoing to be using TOR and Bitcoin on a daily basis from now on, I hope you will keep your online privacy and security in mind and avoid being a victim of either criminals or LE. If you have some knowledge of the basics, you are already better protected than the 90% of the internet users. Better to be paranoid and safe, than lazy and sorry.

I want to thank you for buying this book. If you've found it helpful, I would appreciate it greatly if you could write an honest review to steer others towards it. You can do so here:

https://www.amazon.com/Tor-Dark-Net-Remain-Online-ebook/dp/B01D1SF82W

I wish you the best of luck, and the best security available,

J. Smith

LIKE THIS BOOK?

Check us out online or follow us on social media for exclusive deals and news on new releases!

 https://www.pinnaclepublish.com

 https://www.facebook.com/PinnaclePublishers/

 https://twitter.com/PinnaclePub